The experience
of Ordination

Centre for
Faith and Spirituality
Loughborough University

The experience of Ordination

A SYMPOSIUM BY
Tony Barnard
David Bridge
Donald English
Peter Hebblethwaite
Ruth Matthews
Mary Tanner
Kenneth Wilson

EDITED BY

KENNETH WILSON

LONDON
EPWORTH PRESS

Enquiries should be addressed to
The Methodist Publishing House
Wellington Road
Wimbledon
London SW19 8EU

7162 0324 3

Printed in Great Britain by
The Garden City Press Limited
Letchworth, Hertfordshire SG6 1JS

Contents

Introduction

Anxiety among the clergy has been widespread, since the enthusiasm and confidence of the fifties. This collection of essays approaches the present situation by way of theological autobiography. For it seemed reasonable to suppose that at a time when discussion of 'contextual theology' was so alive, the context of a person's reading and work would have enlivened, or made more exact, an understanding of what it was to be ordained. Anglican, Free Church and Roman Catholic, lay and ordained, were asked and agreed to contribute.

An autobiographical approach has the inevitable danger of repetition, but this is outweighed by the opportunity for freshness and personal experience. And it was obviously right to ask a lay person to reflect too, since it is in the context of the fundamental sacrament of the whole Church, that ordained ministry takes its place. In any case, the laity have a shrewd and special experience of the ordained ministry which must be put alongside a minister's own expectations and experience.

Three vital points arise. The first is that the fundamental sacrament is the Church. The Church was not created by the ordained ministry; rather for the whole purpose of presenting fully the ministry of the Church, the Church has need of those who are ordained. But this priority of the Church has important implications for such things as education and service. The clergy do not carry the learning of the Church for the Church, they stimulate and develop the whole Church's understanding of God, and his work in creation, expressed in the life and teaching of Jesus Christ. To the extent that clergy begin to feel that they are privy to special knowledge, they destroy the fundamental gift of God to the world through Christ, his Church. The corollary of this is that the ordained person cannot restrict his awareness of the world to whatever he chooses to call 'religion'. For if he is to have the capacity and skill to interest the whole Church (and in principle that means all mankind), in the world of God's creation, so that it may be redeemed, he must know something about it. This of course is entirely compatible with the fact that the Church requires scholars in each area of its life.

It is in this context that we should reflect on the sacrament of ordination, and the controversies that have and do reign over whether ordination is ontological, representative or functional. The historical discussion of these points of view is littered with unfairnesses, lies and fears. Our task now is not to decide between them, but to see in what way ordination can be ontological, and representative, and functional. There can, it seems, be no ontological understanding of ordination which is not also representative and functional. A representative view which does not make ontological claims for that which it represents, will be inadequate in its capacity to represent. A functional view which does not assume a representative role will have a restricted view of what that function is. Each of these traditions of reflection has an important contribution to make, which could be developed within the crucial insight that the fundamental sacrament is the sacrament of the Church.

A second point concerns the over-riding importance of theology. There is no discipline easier to ridicule; there is no discipline more necessary to the fullness of the Church's life. Hence it is with some passion that one observes with regret the lack of commitment to theological reflection within the Christian churches. Of course, if theology is confused with, and reduced to, knowing what St Athanasius said, that does make it fair game for ridicule. But why should such ignorance pass for realism, when we should dismiss the confusion of politics with Tudor Administrative History, or economics with accountancy, as arrant nonsense. The tragedy of our situation is that theology is needed in every context in which man attempts to work out the consequences of the fact that this is God's world, and that he is inviting all men to share responsibility for it with him. Hence the essence of theology is the confidence to ask, what does present experience (my experience, your experience, the experience of society, etc.) do to enhance and extend my understanding of what it means to believe in God and his purposes for the world. The opposite seems all too frequently to have been taken as its essence. What disciplines of life and prayer can I develop which will enable me to restrict my experience of life to those which will merely confirm my present understanding of God? We have far too little theology, not too much; the health of Christians, of the Church, and of society at large is the poorer for this.

The various attempts to reduce theology to an aspect of social science, or history, or psychology, need to be seen in this context. It is of course true that all the various disciplines of human enquiry have implications for theological reflection. Thus our increasing understanding of the human brain is of interest, as also the historian's questions regarding the first century, or the physicist's about the nature of energy, or the palaeontologist's about the evolution of the dinosaur. But theology is not neuro-physiology, history, physics, or palaeontology; it is what it is and not another thing. Attempts to defend it, however by making it free from criticism from other disciplines are totally misguided. Such isolation destroys relevance, and the possibility of meaning. An ordained person must be working at this theological task, not because he alone is equipped to do it, but just because if he does not do it, the Church as a whole will be likely to give up the task. And it is a task for the whole Church, to explore the meaning of God's creation, and of man's responsibility within it.

The third point concerns the domestication of the clergy. A tendency with any understanding of the world is to systematize itself, and then to develop institutions which will defend that systematization against change. Such a natural procedure is of questionable value in a time of rapid change, when a quick response and bold thinking are necessary. An irony of the situation for many of those who are set free to serve the Church and to enable it to fulfil the purpose of God for it in the world, is that they discover they were freer when they were lay people. The Church, far from giving them freedom, has domesticated them. By doing so it frustrates its own ministry to the world. It must be clearly understood that I am not here wanting to suggest that the ordained person should not be seen to have an important role within the Church; rather that the way in which he carries it out should not be seen as that of comforter alone, but as stimulator, energizer. He will need to think himself, if he is to do this; he will need to want others to understand; he will have to dare to accept responsibility, if he is to become free. For he must know, that only those who are becoming free, have the resourcefulness and confidence to help others to become free.

I would like to thank the Rev. John Stacey of the Methodist Publishing House, whose interest and encouragement has been of vital importance to the evolution of this book. It is dedicated to the renewal of confidence and optimism amongst mankind, so that God's glory may be recognized and celebrated.

1

Ministry and Ordination
Donald English

The Rev. Donald English was born in the north-east of England. After reading history at London University, and taking a diploma in education at Leicester, he was a Travelling Secretary with the Inter-Varsity Fellowship. He has taught in theological colleges both in England and Nigeria, and at present holds the Lord Rank Chair of Practical Theology and Methodism at Wesley College, Bristol.

He has written, *God in the Gallery, Christian Discipleship* and *Windows on the Passion.* He was elected President of the Methodist Conference in 1978.

Mr English is married, with two sons.

I was three years of age when I first accepted responsibility in the Methodist Church. My onerous task was to pump the organ. The effectiveness of this ministry was measured by the descent of the lead weight on the side of the instrument. As it came down I was winning; if it went up Mr Huntsman the organist was winning. The competition gave to the services not only an interest but an excitement of a kind rarely matched since.

That early experience of ministry provided me with a vantage point from which to observe worship, and here I received my earlier remembered impressions of the People of God. The chapel (this designation is important) was at one end of a country Circuit in the United Methodist Connexion. I have no recollection whatsoever of any ordained minister. Our preachers were laymen. I was baptized by a lay Pastor (though I have no conscious memory of that). At the Lord's Supper the bread and wine were distributed by my uncle Will and my uncle George. My mother and auntie ran the Women's Fellowship. My overall impression, as I look back, is of a community accepting total responsibility for its life and witness. If ordained ministry did play a large part in that activity, it was wholly hidden from me.

Our move as a family to another village led to my involvement in an ex-Primitive Methodist church where again the lay leadership was the clue to the life of the church. We then moved again, and another ex-Primitive church deepened this impression. I was fourteen before involvement in a town chapel in the Wesleyan tradition introduced me to regular pastoral care and observable leadership by an ordained minister. After a significant experience of personal commitment to Church, however, it was lay leadership of a fellowship class and the Sunday School which contributed most to my Christian growth. At university an inter-denominational group, part of the Inter-Varsity Fellowship, provided the setting for further growth—paralleled by the work of the local Methodist church, where the ordained minister exercised an effective ministry to students.

This rather long biographical introduction serves to underline the fact that for me and perhaps for many young Methodists the ordained minister does not figure highly in the beginning or the growth of Christian life. And since it is in the setting of the church that the call to ordained ministry often comes, the prospective candidate for the ministry is prompted by the suggestions of lay people, or by a particular friendship with a minister rather than through the normal life of the church itself. In the former case the candidate finds himself moving towards ordained ministry as the 'most obvious' outlet for the gifts and abilities recognized by fellow Christians who encourage him in that direction. In the latter case it is often a recognition of quality in the minister(s) who befriends him, or a desire to do the things and fulfil the roles which can be *seen* by an observer. In either case, or a combination of the two, certain views of ordained ministry are likely to be uppermost.

The first can be called *charismatic*. A young Christian's growth indicates gifts and abilities within the life of the church, and older Christians observe this. Within his own life he is aware that such potential is best fulfilled in the context of ministry within or on behalf of the church. The pressing question is whether such gifts and abilities are being used to the full in 'secular', 'lay', employment, with limited voluntary involvement in church life. Are God's gifts being properly used in that setting? If the ordained ministry is seen as the obvious outcome of such a situation, then the resultant (because causative) view of ordination will centre on charismatic insights. The routes into the ordained ministry are likely to be those of vocation and personal fulfilment.

Another view is the *functional* one. The church is looking for people to exercise gifts of leadership. The minister's task is seen along certain lines—preaching, visitation, administration. Those who seem capable of such tasks are likely to be pointed in this direction. Friendship with the minister, in a pastoral setting, will highlight particular tasks. It is not only the task-orientation which is significant here; it is the fact that *certain* tasks are highlighted. The view of the essential role of the ordained minister thus exercises a strong influence upon the encouragement and selection of recognizable types of candidate. (A Methodist who shows little promise as a preacher is not likely to be encouraged to offer, for example.)

My own experience was of this kind. Questions of ordained ministry were for me largely questions of vocation (what was God calling me to do with my life?); stewardship (how could the gifts God had given be used to the full in his service?); and fulfilment (which parts of my life gave the greatest sense of doing what I was intended to do?). Materials for answering those questions were my daily bible-reading and prayer, participation in the life of the church, advice from ministers and others about one's suitability, or otherwise, for ordained ministry, reflection upon the logical outcome of one's life, abilities and training so far, and sensitivity to the moments of greatest fulfilment in daily living. In so far as there was any doctrine of ordination involved it was of the functional charismatic kind, since both the church life I knew and the Christian experience I had had raised only that kind of question about ordained ministry. Theologically, Methodist Protestant convictions about the nature of the church and the priesthood of all believers precluded ideas of a separate class of Christians called priests who were ontologically different from the rest.

I therefore went to theological college to train to be a pastor, preacher (one who leads worship and preaches) and administrator. The fact that at that time ministers still largely divided their days to facilitate this threefold task—study in the morning, visiting in the afternoon, meetings in the evening—encouraged such a picture. College training did, of course, raise the question of ordination, but a functional charismatic view was defensible, fitted well into Methodist Deed of Union Statements, and accorded with what I observed in the lives of ministers I knew.

On reflection I can see, though I wasn't very much aware of it at the time, that the first question mark against this as a total view of ordination was raised by a decision of the church about my future. Instead of leaving college to be the pastor/preacher/administrator I wished to be, I was appointed to teach in theological college. After two years of that I was ordained, having been a probationer, passed the necessary examinations and received the appropriate commendations. But I had not functioned in the role I had envisaged, nor would I after ordination, for I was on my way to a theological lectureship overseas. The charismatic element could survive scrutiny. Since I was able and trained as a teacher it would be logical to teach (though why I *needed* to be ordained to do so was not so clear). The functional view was less intact. The trouble was that, by and large, I wasn't functioning in Methodism in the manner understood by that view. (The fact that connexional secretaries and other tutors weren't doing so either was in no sense a solution.) My ordination took place, nevertheless, and I understood it largely in terms of God (both personally and through the church) confirming his call to me and giving me (personally and through the church) the authority to be a minister in the church. From my side it was a re-affirmation of my response to that call, a promise to accept the discipline of God through the church (including appointment to teach the New Testament in Nigeria) and a renewed commitment to God's service. I believed he was giving and would give me the grace I needed. It was therefore a point in a process; a significant culmination of some things and beginning of others. It expressed liturgically and symbolically what I believed to be true and what the church by its action was affirming to be true. Within the boundaries of God's call, the church's confirmation, my response and training, there was a status conferred, a discipline imposed, a promise of strength for the task, and the knowledge of an appointment to be filled. As such the ordination was significant, appropriate and important, though it lacked for me the high emotional tone of the experience of a fellow ordinand who used electrical terms to describe his feelings as hands were laid on him and the words spoken.

Years in theological teaching overseas provided two new influences related to this subject. One was the importance of *status* in African culture. It was not only important, it had to be reflected in dress, station, style of life and protocol. Although the Westerner might be forgiven for feeling that questions of worthiness and efficiency also enter in, there is an obvious security for all involved, and a strong sense of one's place in any situation, when status, rank and honour are given high priority.

The other influence was exerted by representatives of other denominations with whom I worked closely. The acceptance of episcopacy, for example, and the sense of priesthood even among evangelical Anglicans, which differed from most Methodist ideas of ministry, provided new perspectives on one's own views. Pressures for church union were as influential in Nigeria as in England during the same period of time. One had to ask why some fellow-Christians saw things in a different light. Yet one was also committed to defending what one believed to be a true doctrine of ministry against other views which were either contrary to biblical teaching or gave the impression that only one understanding of ministry was defensible on biblical and other grounds. There were two separate problems here. One was the pressure to seek union with all other Christians. The other was how far one could go in accepting a differing view of ministry from one's own as definitive, or how far one should resist such views in the interests of truth. Within a vortex of this kind all one's opinions undergo severe testing. The study of statements of belief, of draft ordinals, of the welter of books, pamphlets and papers which surround both the long discussions with fellow-Christians of a variety of viewpoints, the self-examination of one's own position, convictions and loyalties bring cherished ideas and attitudes under fresh scrutiny.

It is easy, from this vantage point, to give over-clear definitions to insights and convictions which emerged during that period of time in the 1960s and early 70s. But for the sake of clarity some such attempt must be made.

First, one came to see that questions of *order in the church* required a higher place in relation to *the faith of the church* than I had previously allowed. It is easy, raised in what is after all a denomination founded on revival and a deep personal experience, to view formal and institutional discipline as largely unnecessary if only everyone involved would walk with the Lord and obey the Spirit. (Instances of 'hierarchical' heavy-handedness, and of 'bureaucrafts' who are alleged to lack spiritual vigour and insight, encourage such attitudes.)

Judgements of this kind may sound strange coming from a Methodist, recalling the discipline exercised among the earliest of John Wesley's followers. It is important to recall, however, that his discipline was largely a matter of personal discipline exercised by him alone—even in the setting of the early conferences. He was to them a father, not an ecclesiastical dignitary. His authority was based on his own worth, vision, ability and character; not on institutional status. The latter kind of authority arose in Methodism after his death, and the first half of the nineteenth century tells the sad story of divisions and separations as a result (though institutional authority was not the only cause of unrest during those years). Nevertheless, just as the Methodist way to improve worship is not traditionally to alter the liturgy but to call the congregation to examine its heart before God, so there is a tendency in Methodism to view with suspicion all hierarchical and institutional figures—save perhaps one, the President, whom it has chosen, who lasts for one year only, and whose power obviously attaches to the office rather than to the person.

During the hectic years of union debate in Nigeria, then, after my return, in England, I came to attach greater significance to order than hitherto; and to formal structures for achieving and preserving order. Within such structures the question of office and status naturally arises, and I learned at that time to face the fact that in the New Testament Church status *did* matter, and that St Paul himself was not averse to calling for obedience because of the status of apostle which he claimed for himself. This was not a new discovery for me, of course, but it received a 'higher rating' in my categories of thought about ministry than hitherto. Thus episcopacy expressed through an episcopate (historic or otherwise) did not of itself hold for me a threat, by contrast with our Methodist leadership titles of President, Chairman and Superintendent, which all carry functional rather than status connotations, both by their exercise and by their impermanence.

It was within this setting that I was able to see the ordained minister in more than a functional and charismatic light. Another possible perspective saw him as having a status within an ordered system of church life, *representing* divine authority and church authority within the church and to the world outside the church.

On the other side, however, certain balancing convictions were hardened, and some of them are inextricably linked.

I found myself rejecting more strongly than ever the idea that any one structure of ministry—the threefold order of bishop, priest, deacon was a case in point—could be shown to be unquestionably required by biblical teaching for the life of the modern church, even if it could be shown to be universally accepted and practised in the New Testament Church, which I doubt. One could only judge that if this was the form of ministry which the New Testament writers wished to record and advocate as of universal application to the life of the church in their time and ours then they did a bad job. Nor were the claims being made for this particular form of ministry, in particular the historic episcopate, self-evidently true. The attempt therefore, as a matter of divine purpose, to impose such a form of ministry upon all the churches was both improper (in my judgement) and was based, as I heard Professor C. K. Barrett say some years ago, on bad theology and bad history. It is bad theology because the biblical basis for it is inadequate. It is bad history because there is too little evidence for the nature of its origin and continuity, and too much evidence for its failure to achieve precisely what it alone is said to preserve in the life and witness of the church.

That there were biblical principles of Christian ministry which were and are essential to the life of the church was something of which I became increasingly certain. That particular offices or structures invariably had preserved or were intended to preserve such principles in every place at every age of the church I doubted, and doubt very strongly.

Perhaps more basically still I came during those years of union negotiations to mistrust an emphasis which involved safeguarding the ordained ministry as a way of safeguarding the life of the church. Too much of the union material was concerned exclusively with questions of ordained ministry. Of course it can be argued that these were the major centres of controversy between the denominations, but this reply merely pushes the question one step further back. Why *must* it be the case that when sacraments are discussed the debate inevitably and unerringly moves on to questions of ordained ministry? They are not, after all, the preserve of the ordained. Or have they become so? And if so, is this healthy? Why was it that at every stage the dialogue about major elements in the life of the church—worship, initiation, sacraments, preaching, discipline, legislation—turned into disagreements about ordained ministry? It seemed increasingly clear to me that this was the result of the error of 'defining the church by its clergy'; of making the 'ordained ministry' the focal point and essential element in the life of the church. To the argument that these issues dominate our union discussions because they are precisely the points of difference one can only reply that the debate should be about the presuppositions and developments which have caused them to be the markers of divergence instead of the rallying points of reconcilation. The indications seemed to be that the ordained ministry had become altogether too exclusive, powerful and normative within the life of the church. In so becoming it had often stifled the spiritual growth and effectiveness of the non-ordained Christian family—as books like *God's Frozen People* lamented.

Such convictions were strengthened for me by my experience of circuit ministry (at last), and my theological reflections after returning to theological college work (again). Other convictions, however, have grown up alongside them during those years.

In circuit I served a large and flourishing suburban church and a small and struggling church on a council estate. In both situations I found myself becoming clearer on two separate issues. One concerned the context of evaluating the meaning of ordained ministry. The other concerned the nature of the ordained minister's task.

As far as context was concerned, it was increasingly borne in upon me in circuit that the ministry of the whole church was the major setting in which to consider ordained ministry. This was not the first time such thoughts had occurred to me, but they were now reinforced unmistakably by my life in circuit. My particular stations surrounded me with many devout, able and active lay Christians. The life of both churches was warm, spiritual and issued in service to each neighbourhood. My ministry was meaningful as it overlapped and complemented that of my lay brothers and sisters. My ministry as an ordained person did not give theirs its authority or validity any more than theirs did mine. Both—all—types of ministry, lay and ordained, were authorized and validated by God, and in such a setting it became possible properly to view the Body of Christ in that place, and properly to assess the meaning of one's ordained ministry.

Understanding one's ordained ministry as one part of the total ministry of the church, and not as superior or inferior to any other part, had a number of significant results. One was, for example, being free to be ministered to, by laymen, as well as to minister to them. In meetings with church stewards I experienced very deep fellowship and received, as well as exercised, ministry. Such a view also facilitated and helped to create a sense of teamwork in the life of the church. Hierarchical structures, with the ordained minister at the apex of the triangle, were not the framework within which we operated. Individuals and committees were free to get on with their work without my authorization, supervision or checking. It was, after all, as much their church as mine (in fact it is God's!), and when I had moved on many of them would still be there. God's call, not my presence, validated their work. And I was free to make mistakes. The minister need not be viewed as the best Christian around, any more than he ought to be viewed as omnicompetent. Mine was not a superior ministry, but a different one.

The greatest difficulty arising from such a method of assessing ordained ministry is, of course, to identify where precisely the difference lies between this and lay ministry. It is difficult simply to isolate one activity or another in a purely functional way. Preaching, visiting, administration, counselling, teaching are all done by lay people, some of whom are better at it than some ministers. Lay people, baptize, though exceptionally rather than as a rule. Ministers marry and make members, though in the latter case for Methodists the significant moment is not the service of confirmation but the vote of the Church Council, almost all of whom are lay, that the persons should be members. The Minister presides at the Lord's Supper, yet lay people are increasingly sharing parts of that ministry, and some lay people are given authorization by the Methodist Conference to preside in exceptional circumstances. It is not easy to establish the difference on a functional basis alone. There are few things an ordained minister does which no lay Christians do. He does not necessarily do all these things more than lay Christians do. Some retired lay Christians *may* do more visiting; some professionally or voluntarily may do more counselling; some undoubtedly do more church administration. It is difficult to see how any lay person could do more preaching than the average circuit minister, but in other denominations it might just be possible. The one major functional distinction is that while most of the minister's tasks are performed by one lay person or another, generally only he does them all, and is authorized and expected to do them all. (The expectation is not so great where ministers are appointed to administrative or teaching posts, but they are exceptions.)

Similar problems exist in connection with the charismatic view of ordained ministry. That certain gifts are required for such a calling is generally accepted. It is likely, therefore, that ordained ministers will differ from *some* lay people in possessing such gifts. But who would argue that *all* Christians who *are* so gifted *will* be called into ordained ministry? And who would be courageous (or foolhardy) enough to draw up a list of minimum gifts required as essential qualifications for ordained ministry? And to what extent or in which balance are these gifts to be possessed and exercised? This way of establishing the difference between ordained and lay simply will not do. Apart from being unworkable as a criterion it comes dangerously close to limiting God's sovereignty in calling men and women into ordained ministry.

This kind of argument does not dispense with functional and charismatic views of ministry as important ways of viewing ordination. Nor are they wholly irrelevant to the question of boundaries between lay and ordained. But they cannot stand alone in establishing such boundaries.

It is at this point that one returns to the idea of the minister as a *representative person*. Such a view does not exclude functional and charismatic approaches. In fact it needs them. They provide a context of work done and persons gifted to do it. They also safeguard representative ordination against becoming something purely private and inward rather than something evidenced in life and work.

The exact nature of this representative element needs defining with great care, however. After all, every Christian 'represents' the Christian church and the Christian gospel.

People expect a Christian to know and believe what Christians believe, to live as Christians live, to go to church as Christians do, and to adopt the attitudes which Christians adopt—though all within broad limits. What is more, they judge the church by the Christians. In this sense we cannot avoid being representatives—all of us.

Yet some lay Christians are viewed as 'more representative than others'. An office holder, for example, is viewed as more representative of the church, or as representative in a different way, by both Christians and non-Christians. He exercises leadership within the church and is therefore expected to know more about its life. Christians of his persuasion will take a lead from him, ask advice of him, perhaps even model themselves upon him. They are not limited to leaders for any such help, of course, but there is an appropriateness and an expectation where leaders are concerned because, by reason of appointment, ability and status, they are representatives. In that sense they sum up, in themselves, by position and function, what is in fact true of all the church.

People outside the church make a distinction between the representative nature of lay leaders and the function of all Christians in representing Christianity. Yet leadership representation differs in degree rather than kind from the rest, and it is not exclusive.

A similar case can be made out for the representative nature of ordained ministry. Christians and non-Christians expect a level of representation by reason of the status of the ordained minister. Moreover, the nature of his representative status *is* different. The ordained minister has sensed a 'call' from God, has submitted to scrutiny and selection, training and testing, discipline and duty in a system leading to ordination. This system, in its combined parts and as a whole, is different from all other processes within the church. The nature of the minister's commitment is different, too, in terms of the discipline accepted and the role adopted. In all of these senses he is a representative of the church in a way which lay people are not. Moreover, the ordained minister gathers up all the representative functions in himself (or herself) though not in the sense that others do not perform them.

The major question is whether this representation is

different in degree or kind from that of the lay Christian. Could the line not just as easily be drawn between Christians who do not hold office and those who do (including lay and ordained)? Or should this kind of line be drawn anyway? Putting it more traditionally, is ordained ministry Christ's gift to the church, in a particular sense, or is it one of many gifts to the church, including all that lay people do within its life? Is it Christ's gift *to* the church, or one of his many gifts *from within* it? Can it—or ought it—in any sense to be viewed apart from the church, or always and only within it?

The Methodist Church seems to me to come down clearly on the second of these ways of expressing the matter, saying of its ordained ministers that 'they hold no priesthood differing in kind from that which is common to all the Lord's people and they have no exclusive title to the preaching of the gospel or the care of souls. These ministries are shared with them by others to whom also the Spirit divides His gifts severally as He wills.' A little later the Deed of Union adds 'The Methodist Church holds the doctrine of the priesthood of all believers and consequently believes that no priesthood exists which belongs exclusively to a particular order or class of men but in the exercise of its corporate life and worship special qualifications for the discharge of special duties are required and thus the principle of representative selection is recognised.' In these statements the charismatic, functional and representative elements are all clearly to be observed. This does not mean that the ordained minister is solely, or even primarily, answerable to an institution. 'Christ's Ministers in the Church are Stewards in the household of God and Shepherds of His flock.' They are Christ's Ministers, and as such are Stewards and Shepherds, answerable to God, whose household and flock they care for. Yet all others who 'minister' in the Church are equally called and answerable.

The way in which a balance can be achieved in practice within the Church is indicated by examination of another way of assessing ordained ministry, so far alluded to, but not specifically outlined. This is the *vocational* element. The Methodist Deed of Union stresses this way of viewing ordained ministry. 'It is the universal conviction of the Methodist people that the office of the Christian Ministry depends upon the call of God . . .' Yet the individual's sense of and claim to such a call is not of itself sufficient ground for being ordained. Thus God 'bestows the gifts of the Spirit, the grace and the fruit which indicate those whom He has chosen'. Those who are ordained 'by the imposition of hands' are those 'whom the Methodist Church recognises as called of God'.

In this way the prevenience of God's call is preserved. But the individual's sense of call is tested by the Church and in the light of God's gifts of grace and fruit of the Spirit for the fulfilment of the task. It may be that it is around this centre that some kind of consensus about ordained ministry might emerge.

Arising from such a consideration, though not wholly dependent upon it, is the question of authority. For the ordained minister it has at least two separate parts. One is the nature of his authority *within* the Church; the other is the nature of his authority, as a minister, in the world *outside* the Church. In particular those engaged in forms of service and caring.

Within the Church the model of authority has for centuries reflected attitudes to authority in the community at large. Pyramidal structures have been upheld and used in government, business, armed forces and families for centuries. At the apex of the triangle stands—or perhaps more appropriately, sits—the figure with greatest authority, be he prime minister, managing director, general or father. When such an authority structure is applied to the Church, the apex figure is the minister or priest. Such authority is confirmed by the tendency to view him as a professional Christian, leading amateurs whose professional status is enjoyed at work but not in the church. If the minister leads all or most of the services and chairs all or most of the meetings then the pyramid shape of ecclesiastical authority in the local church is still further reinforced.

Each of the views of ordination adumbrated so far in this chapter can be advanced to support such an authority structure. In functional terms 'it is his job'. On a charismatic interpretation 'he does it so well'. From the representative point of view 'it is his rightful position'. It is not surprising that such a system has operated fairly widely in all the churches for a long time—and often with commendable success.

Three considerations, however, provide grounds for unease about such a situation. The first and most obvious is the changed attitude towards authority in our culture at the present time. If being bracketed with the squire and the schoolmaster as the third bastion of authority used to be a source of strength to the minister, it is rarely so these days. In our modern society authority is not so much conferred as earned. Readiness by one person to assume authority has always required willingness on the part of others to recognize and accept its exercise over them. This is not new. But previously it was seen as appropriate for the squire, the schoolmaster and the minister to claim authority. Therefore people were willing to submit to its exercise over them by such professions. This is now much less the case. The ordained ministry has suffered from the steady erosion of 'statutory' authority (alongside most other professions).

At this point the functional and representative views of ordination are likely to be less helpful than the charismatic. As authority is detached from status the ministers right to function as head of every activity will be (and *is* currently) called in question. The functional approach is thus seen to be a plank of the very platform which is being dismantled.

Nor is the representative perspective much more successful. To claim authority because one represents the wider body within the church is easily turned into a defence of the pyramid which is no longer accepted. Why should the ordained minister be the authoritative person who represents the Church at large in every aspect of the life of the local church? Does ordination automatically establish the minister at this apex point in every sphere? If it *is* so viewed, then why is it? If it is not, then why are so many ministers expected to operate as though it were?

It is the charismatic approach which is most likely to prevail in an atmosphere where authority has to be earned rather than assumed. It may be the general quality of the minister's life, it may be the exercise of particular gifts, it may be the visionary and prophetic nature of his leadership, which inspires people to acknowledge and accept his authority. Where these qualities are lacking it is much less likely that they will do so in the modern climate of opinion.

For many modern Christians this development will be a

welcome one. A charismatic view of ordination brings with it a charismatic view of lay Christianity too. Alongside the ordained minister's gifts one must place the gifts of the lay member of the church. If the minister is not regarded as having authority in a given area of the life of the church, because he is not gifted in that area, it is likely that some of his lay people will be so gifted and will be seen as possessing and exercising authority at that point. The church is thus seen to operate as a body, each playing his or her part—both ordained and lay—and each exercising whatever authority goes with the gift exercised. The one head of such a body is Jesus Christ and there is no one intermediary.

Such a picture is not as complete as it seems, however, nor a total solution to the problem either. Can an ordained minister's authority ever be gauged by the extent of his gifts and the effectiveness of his exercise of them? Is authority in any institution capable of being measured in this quantitive way? And even if it were, by whom would it be so measured? Who determines the extent or effectiveness of an ordained minister's gifts and allocates authority accordingly? Then there is the important consideration that God has given to his Church not only *ordained ministers* but also *ordained ministry*. Each minister represents not only his own life and work but also a wider entity of which he is only a part. It must be seriously doubted whether the charismatic view, with its particularist and individualistic tendencies, provides adequately for a holist view of ordained ministry, though it understandably does in its view of the local church, with the ordained ministry operating alongside all other ministries.

A second major source of unease about pyramidal structures of authority with the ordained minister at the apex is the way in which such a pattern masks the servant nature of the ministry. After all, 'minister' does mean 'servant'. And although an ordained minister may feel that he is primarily *God's* servant, we do think and speak of him as 'ministering' to *people*. 'Your servant for Christ's sake' was St Paul's way of expressing it. However the minister may feel about it, if he sits at the top of a hierarchical authority structure he will experience a disturbing conflict of roles and attitudes.

Here the functional view of ordination may prove least helpful. Structures can determine fuction. Charismatic insight may or may not clarify the situation, depending upon the gifts of the minister. The representative view is most likely to ensure some tolerable resolution of inevitable tension. Authority in leadership and meetings, in services and teaching, does not need to rely upon a structure with a certain shape. It can be seen as depending upon a certain person, after appropriate selection, training and testing, being recognized as holding authority as a representative of the Church, and of Jesus Christ in the Church. Such a person need not be at the top of every ladder, not in the chair at every meeting, nor in the seat of honour at every function. His authority does not rest in such a system, nor need such bolstering up for its exercise. Neither does it hinder a 'servant ministry' nor feel threatened by one. This combination of authority and service, so clearly seen in Jesus Christ, is a crucial element in all the ordained ministry.

The third origin of unease about authority depending upon hierarchy is the nature of grace. In biblical teaching grace is essentially an offer not a command. It is also vulnerable rather than protected. The death of Jesus Christ on the Cross is the supreme example of this. If the ordained minister is to be a representative of such grace he must himself demonstrate its characteristics. At this point it is none of the three views outlined—functional, charismatic and representative—which provides the clue. It is the *nature of the call* to ordained ministry. Such a call comes to those who have already experienced God's grace in Christ, or how else could they or why else would they be called? And the call itself comes *as* grace. It is an offer of a part of the Lord's purposes for his Church in the world. As such it is vulnerable. It can be ignored, neglected or rejected. It is true that to ignore, neglect or reject grace is to diminish oneself, but the essential vulnerability of grace is not removed by that aspect of reality and experience. What is more, he who responds to the call must live by grace. He not only proclaims good news of God's grace: he lives on the strength of such good news. His exercise of authority must be all of a piece with the message he proclaims and the life-style he follows.

Authority which grows out of grace is a risky business. For it offers, rather than imposes itself. It is essentially vulnerable. It has no props to lean upon. Its availability, its exercise and its acceptance by others all operate within the area of grace and on the basis of its presuppositions. A minister who exercises authority in this way will be constantly driven back to Christ as his pattern and the Lord as his strength.

The picture of ordained ministry which emerges thus far is a varied and many sided one. It does not depend on one view but on several. Each will provide its own perspectives and dimensions. They will in turn be more or less important, depending upon the circumstances and their requirements. But all are required for a whole picture, and each will find its source and pattern in Jesus Christ himself.

I end by noting two developments in the exercise of ordained ministry. One I regret, the other I commend though I discern little evidence of it in the Church today.

The development I *regret* is what I would call a 'ministry of the gaps'. It operates only in those areas of life which are as yet untouched or uncontrolled by the growing influence of social and health care. Wherever official help is not available, such ministry is present. Thus the minister squeezes into the steadily decreasing space allowed for him by the psychiatrist, doctor, social worker and other of the 'caring' and 'serving' professions. Such space is not only decreasing, it is becoming distinctly cramped. A corollary of this situation is the number who leave neighbourhood ministry to join the professions listed above in order to have a 'man-size' job. (Of course not all who make such a move do so for this reason, and still fewer would express it in this way.)

That ministers should operate in the areas untouched by provisions of the Welfare State is not in doubt. But that such should be the *limit* of such ministry must be strongly denied. Such a situation is not only a diminution of ministry. It diminishes Christian theology and ultimately one's vision of God.

In practical terms ordained ministry is required not only to visit the sick in hospital and home but also to have a theological understanding of persons, health and human responsibility which enables comment upon the entire system of health care in our country. We need not only a proper exercise of charity to those in need but also discernment of those injustices in theory, relationships and structures which give rise to the needs. And we require a passion for justice and righteousness which spills out beyond the areas of 'churchly activity' into the whole area of life around us. Most of all we need a theological understanding of man and his environment in relation to God which enables others to see that there is more to man's nature and needs than can be supplied by social and welfare agencies. From this point of view theology is not simply one academic discipline alongside many others, taking its chance with the rest. It is the understanding of God which sheds light upon all other disciplines; that response to God which provides perspective on all life's relationships, that perception of reality which puts one in touch with the meaning of existence. Ministry based upon such understanding can never be limited to other people's gaps. Its purview is all of life, lived by all people in all places.

The development I *look* for concerns the minister as theologian. There is in most denominations a fairly well-set pattern of expectation where the work of the ordained minister is under discussion. He is pastor, preacher, administrator, man of prayer, and a variety of other things. Different traditions have different emphases, but in the main a fairly common picture emerges. Congregations, by their expectations, exert considerable influence upon their ministers to conform to the pattern. Few seem to expect him to be a theologian.

Part of the reason for this lack of expectation may be the associations of theology for many Christians. It represents for them an academic, difficult, esoteric discipline, pursued by the highly educated, often to the detriment of Christian faith and assurance. Such Christians find theological books difficult to read, theological fashions as transitory as any other, and theological preachers boring and unintelligible. Their cry is for simpler preaching and teaching, easier to understand and more related to everyday life.

At the level of academic theology many such criticisms would be valid in the setting of worship and Christian instruction. The professional, academic theologian is not concerned about the influence of his latest theory upon the congregations up and down the country. His task is to use the resources at his disposal to push back the barriers of ignorance as far as possible in as disinterested a manner as possible.

Yet the faith of the people of God is important. Their experience of him in every day life, their search for truth within their experience, their knowledge gained by a variety of activities is also significant for theology.

My plea for ministers as theologians is probably therefore a plea for ministers as theological interpreters. The gap between the academic theologian and the church member is already too wide and seems to be growing. We need generations of ministers who can understand both and be agents of communication across the gap. Otherwise we stand in grave danger of academic theology losing its essential link with the exercise of faith: while the faith of the Church may lose its vital core of intellectual fibre and vigour. To stand between the two, not as umpire but as living link, is no easy task. The ordained ministers are not the only ones who can exercise such a ministry, but they above all are required to do so.

In order to fulfil this function their grasp of both sides of the divide will need to be strong. There will be the necessity to discover again and again the truth that the most lasting theology is done on one's knees. It is an exercise in 'exploring with awe', but there will also be the requirement to worship with one's mind; using all one's intellectual powers to grasp even the fringes of God's being. And there is the task of seeing divine reality in its relationship to daily life. To stand with one foot in the bible and one in the twentieth-century world and to take the strain by standing on both feet is not easy calling. Yet God's people need help to do so, and it is part of the service rendered by the ordained ministry—perhaps the major service, for it permeates every part of the minister's task as it is more popularly viewed. As pastor, preacher, administrator, person of prayer, the minister will need deep theological insight if the ministry is to be grounded in God and in the realities of daily living.

Books I have found helpful
Barrett, C. K., *The Signs of an Apostle,* Epworth 1970
Brandon, Owen, *The Pastor and His Ministry* SPCK 1972
Greeves, Frederic, *Theology and the Cure of Souls,* Epworth 1960
Hanson, Anthony T., *The Church of the Servant,* SCM 1962

Harvey, A. E., *Priest or President?*, SPCK 1975
Küng, Hans, *Why Priests?*, Fontana 1972
Porterhouse, Clive, (ed.), *Ministry in the Seventies*, Falcon 1970
Stibbs, Alan, *God's Church*, IVF 1959
Thornton, Martin, *My God*, Hodder and Stoughton 1974

2

The Ministry
David Bridge

David Bridge was born in Leigh, Lancashire, in 1937 and he has spent most of his life in Methodist manses. He was educated at Kingswood School, and subsequently at Leeds and Manchester Universities. He trained for the ministry at Hartley Victoria College, and obtained the certificate in Ecumenical Studies at the University of Geneva. He is at present the minister of the Cullercoats Methodist Church, North Shields, having previously served in Heald Green, Chester, and Newcastle-under-Lyme. He is happily married with two daughters.

His writings include a book on Leisure, and articles for various periodicals on his two favourite subjects, preaching and the cinema. He is a member of the British Film Institute's Lecture Panel.

Beginnings

Though there is no particular event or experience associated in my mind with becoming a Christian, I well remember the moment at which I decided I wanted to be a Methodist minister. There was nothing remarkable or unusual about it, indeed looking back it seems absurdly traditional and prosaic. During a sermon in the Kingswood School chapel the preacher, the Rev. Kenneth Waights, referred to the ministry and said that perhaps someone present might feel that it was the job for them. It simply struck me for the first time that perhaps this was the job for me.

As far as I can recall my motives at the time, they seem to be so unworthy and inappropriate that it is hard to describe them without some embarrassment. I think I wanted very much to be a Christian but had always feared that the appeal of worldliness would prove too attractive. Now it seemed to me that being a minister would strengthen my feeble resolve to be a Christian. If it was the right thing for me subsequently to be ordained a minister this was, to say the least, an unprepossessing start. I have always found great comfort in the words of Father George Tyrell: 'If one realized what a priest should be, no-one would ever get ordained. God has to be content with such rubbish as he gets.'

As my great-great-grandfather was Ambrose Kirkland, a Primitive Methodist minister, and as there has been a minister in the family in every generation since, it no doubt appeared to many that there was a degree of inevitability about my offering for the ministry, rather like entering the family business. Partly to resist such expectations I had developed a strong antipathy to the idea of being a minister and remember responding sharply to one visitor to our home who asked

indulgently if I was a future President of the Conference—'Not likely—Vice-President, perhaps.' (The Vice-
President of the Methodist Conference is always a lay person.) I had a great love and respect for my father, and thought
highly of his former college friends who used to visit our home
from time to time. Nevertheless, I blamed on my father's job
the fact that I could not play with him as often as I wished (not
yet being aware that many jobs prevent fathers from spending
all the time they would like with their families) and at fifteen
the prospect of spending my life in genteel poverty was unap-
pealing. My clear intention had been to become a barrister
and I used to spend many hours of my school holidays in the
public gallery of the Leeds Crown Court. The decision to
offer for the ministry took me very much by surprise. I think
my father also feared the motive was 'the family business', for
he received my news with apparent indifference, though pri-
vately he told my mother how happy he would be if I should
persist in this intention and it should turn out to be a genuine
call.

At the time I made the decision to offer for the ministry I
had virtually no experience of public speaking and indeed the
idea terrified me. I thought of the ministry purely in terms of
helping people and though I realized in a vague way that it
would involve preaching I remember being under the impression that at some point I should go to college and be
taught how to do it. If I had known then that before entering a
college a student minister has to be a fully qualified lay
preacher, to have preached three trial sermons and written a
fourth, I might well have abandoned the enterprise there and
then. Any sense of a call to preach only came to me much later
and I well remember being asked by my minister at the time,
the Rev. Tom Meadley, what I intended to preach about and
having to answer that I hadn't the faintest idea. This was
precisely true; I had nothing to say, and my first sermons were
wholly plagiarized. I think I had been preaching for two or
three years before I began to have any real idea of what the
Christian faith was about. I cannot interpret or justify this; I
simply report what now seems to me quite plainly to have
been the case.

Having no real idea of what a minister was and no inner
resources of my own from which to construct a blueprint or

model, I began to search in some desperation for whatever models might be available. There was in a sense no shortage and though they turned out to be quite inadequate it is hard to see who or what could be blamed for this. Had there been more realistic models to hand, however, both the church and I might have been spared some of the pain and confusion which my first stumbling attempts to be a minister inevitably provoked, and it is to the search for more appropriate models of ministry that this essay is in the main devoted.

Early Days in Training
My father died when I was just sixteen so I was denied what would have been a most valuable source of help, regular contact and conversation with a practising minister who believed in the importance of what he was doing. I had very vivid memories of him of course, but as memories are frozen while the real world changes these memories were to prove a mixed blessing to a young man starting from scratch to discover what a minister might be. During my teens my whole experience of the church apart from the school chapel was my home church in Leeds. There the morning congregation averaged 250 while the evening congregation was over 1,000. On the occasion of the Chapel Anniversary a weekday lunchtime service would draw 1,500 while the afternoon and evening rallies packed in 2,000. When my family moved to Longton in the Potteries the situation at the Central Hall there was similar. I thought that all churches were like this or at least I never thought about any that were not.

It was clear, to me at least, what a minister was in all this. He was the person who held the whole show together. He was the person whose preaching drew in the crowds and whose special appeals sent up the collection. He was the person whose presence at every gathering, from the Passion Play to the faith tea, was essential if the event was to have real significance. He was a person who could be criticized behind his back but never to his face. He was a person to whom it was impossible to say no. The only popular illusion I did not share was the one about a minister's hours of work. I knew he was never at home.

My experience as a lay preacher and as a theological student was as a result punctuated by a series of rude awakenings. I went with a team of preachers into the York-shire Dales to help a hard-pressed circuit there, and found myself preaching to a congregation of four. I had no idea that such situations existed and was certainly not prepared to cope with them if they did. In the event I pretended that they were 400 and carried on accordingly. They must have thought I was a very strange young man. At least they paid polite attention, which was not always the case. In a village chapel in Cheshire where I went to preach during my first month at college, the organist and organ-blower, sat within eight yards of the pul-pit, shared a bag of sweets during the first prayer and for the rest of the service read the Sunday paper, pausing only to point out to each other items of special interest. I began to feel uncomfortable having to disturb them by announcing a hymn. Looking back I suppose it was good practice for doing tele-vision epilogues.

During college training the search for ministerial models intensifies as students try to relate their training to the sort of people they hope to be at the end of it. Apart from one's pre-college experience what else was available? The college tutors themselves provide the most easily accessible models, but though without exception they were fine and wonderful people, many remaining my friends to this day, their experi-ence of the circuit ministry was usually so far back in the past as to disqualify them for being other than models of college tutors. The idea that circuit ministers might have a part in training future circuit ministers was, and apparently still is, considered to be quite absurd. We were left then with a variety of models from the myths of early Methodism. I shall try and recall a few of these.

(a) *The dynamic preacher.* This version harmonized well with my previous experience. He is the one whose powerful oratory both in the pulpit and the open air attracts the crowds, reviving weak causes and leading strong ones to even greater glories.

(b) *The super social worker.* The Central Missions still had a romantic air about them and we used to revel in the biog-raphies of the great men of the turn of the century who had organized soup kitchens for the deserving poor, spent their evenings picking drunks out of the gutter, and rescued innumerable young women from lives of easy virtue. As evidence that this tradition was not dead we were occasionally visited at college by ministers whose lives seemed to be composed entirely of dangerous encounters with ex-prisoners, prostitutes and meths drinkers.

(c) *The jolly good fellow*. As it was obviously important to be loved by one's people we were duly impressed by the ministers who seemed to have the capacity for the non-stop generation of goodwill, greeting everyone by name with a hearty handshake and a cheery word. The best of these seemed able to address a room of people simultaneously and yet leave each with the impression that they had been spoken to personally. This was a gift I never mastered. They also had an unlimited supply of very funny stories and had their humour not been sanctified by grace they would without doubt have made a very good living as nightclub comedians. Indeed it was rumoured that one or two did.

(d) *The 'troubler of Israel'*. This particular myth was reinforced by some who had recently left college and who would return to tell us that the church was hopelessly out of date and reactionary and quite unworthy of the bright new generation of ministerial students, whose only hope would be to empty the churches of the fuddy-duddies at present in them in order to make room for people who would be more receptive to our particular gifts. They would enthrall us with tales of mighty battles against obdurate trustees and the confounding of incompetent stewards.

However inspiring these particular models were, they also seemed a bit daunting to those who were inclined to timidity or who were less than wholly convinced of the sufficiency of their personal gifts. I turned therefore to the obituary pages in the *Minutes of Conference* for some clues as to the nature of the ministry I was shortly to enter. It was soon apparent that though there were variations of detail, the best ministers had a number of qualities in common. They were brothers beloved, held in high regard by their colleagues. They read widely and possessed well-stored minds. They were wise administrators and diligent pastors. Apart from their wives they did not appear to have any interest outside their work, or if they had the obituarist did not think the fact worth recording.

We also read or had read to us with suitable exhortation the

'Liverpool Minutes', the closest we ever got to a formal model of our ministry. The 'Liverpool Minutes' are a set of resolutions on the nature of the pastoral office first approved by the Wesleyan Conference of 1820, later revised, and printed along with the Methodist Constitution as one of its historic documents. The over-riding impression given by these minutes is of single-minded devotion to the work. The minister is urged to guard against all occupations of time and thought which have no direct relation to his great calling. He is to regard as an evil the practice of visiting or receiving friends on a Sunday even if this does not clash with worship, and he is even to discourage 'local and subordinate enterprises or works of charity' as these lead to the neglect of the public preaching of the gospel, the prayer meeting and the class meeting. To turn from the 'Liverpool Minutes' to the report of the 1977 Conference on the Pastoral Care of the Ministry which urges ministers to cultivate a hobby and to take a whole day off each week and five weeks holiday a year, is to move into an entirely different world. A good antidote to too much heady idealism however was the period of training spent in the circuits, sharing in the life of a circuit minister. Some of the people I met in this way have stayed in my mind ever since as models of the kind of minister I should like to be.

I left college then with a fairly clear idea what a minister was during the nineteenth century but a rather hazy notion of what he might be at the present time. He was clearly someone who stood at the centre of the church, as the whole operation hinged on his abilities. Where he was in the community I never even thought to ask. Certain skills were going to be very important; preaching, the ability to get on with people, the manipulation of business meetings, not to mention the ability to live on very little without grumbling. There were other skills of which I was dimly aware but which I was sure I had not got and and hoped never to be called upon to use, such as leading a soul to Christ, assuring a guilty sinner of repentance having first convicted him of sin, and chastising the back-sliders. I knew these things were important because my Primitive Methodist forbears set great store by them, but I felt that somehow they had been omitted from my training.

40

Learning from Experience

From the moment a minister takes up his first appointment, whatever models he has been able to fashion for himself previously are overwhelmed, sometimes temporarily and sometimes permanently, by an even more powerful set of models, namely the expectations of his congregation and to a lesser extent of the community. These will vary according to the circumstances; I note my own experiences and something of what colleagues have shared with me. In general, however, the expectations of the congregation are that the minister will sustain and develop the work of the local church while the community expects the minister to perform the few vestigial functions of the church which have still not been taken over by secular agencies. In particular these are what sociologists call the 'rites of passage', baptisms, weddings and funerals.

I had managed to leave college without the least idea of what happened at a funeral, and conducted my first, a cremation, entirely by watching the undertaker's eyes. Where he seemed to expect me to go, I went. I took no chances with the second, a burial, and rang a colleague for advice in advance. Weddings were more straightforward, though as a single man at the time I felt that any words of counsel I might give would be regarded as highly suspect. In talking with a couple about their forthcoming wedding, or with parents about a baptism, I became aware of a sharp contrast between the expectations of worshipping members of the church and of others. The second group regarded me in varying degrees as part of the provisions of the welfare state and in a number of instances strongly resented my attempts to behave as anything else. Couples who had asked for Christian marriage were amazed that I should ask if they were Christians. Parents who had planned an afternoon baptism so that Granny could travel from Liverpool were put out at being told that baptisms took place in the context of a normal service so that the congregation might be there to play their part. A mother told me that she had made a christening cake and that as it would be absurd to have a cake for lunch the baptism would have to be in the afternoon. I suppose every minister devises his own technique for coping with the family who will not turn off the television during a baptism interview. Some stand with their backs to the set, but my method was to drop my voice until it was quite impossible for me to be heard above 'Coronation Street' or whatever. There would come a point at which the sight of my lips moving to the sound of Elsie Tanner would strike even the most insensitive as being incongruous.

There was the expectation from members of the church that the minister would visit them in their homes and after a couple of months would know them all by name. Even among church members, however, there were varied expectations about what a minister might actually do when he called. Some looked on his visits as a seal of respectability to which as paid-up Methodists they were fully entitled. The sick and housebound naturally welcomed a visit as a sign that they were still members of the church family. Some appreciated the offering of prayer in the home; others looked alarmed at the suggestion of prayer as if it were a sign that their illness were more serious than they thought. Sometimes the conversation led naturally to a discussion of the Christian life and personal faith, but some would talk easily about every topic except these—the ones on which the minister might be presumed to be the most qualified. There seemed to be a strong expectation that the minister would want to visit the sick rather than the whole. Some people told me not to bother to visit them so that I might have more time for the sick, which revealed a lot about their expectation of a minister. When I replied that I was really interested in getting to know them as people whether they were ill or not, this was received as a highly novel suggestion. Nevertheless, to be approachable and 'human' was clearly a very important qualification.

Thirdly, there were the expectations of a minister as a speaker. People expect that he will preach on a Sunday and be able to speak interestingly at a wide variety of functions during the week. It struck me within a few months of entering the circuit ministry that this expectation amounted to an obsession in certain quarters and I had to learn quickly to distinguish between those who were inviting me because I was a speaker and those who were inviting me to say something. This distinction may seem fanciful to those unacquainted with church life but it is an important one. Each organization has a programme secretary who starts with a blank diary and a number of dates for which he or she has to find speakers. It matters not what the subject is, there is rarely any coherent pattern to the programme, all that is required of the speaker is that he should be able to 'give a few words' or, as one programme secretary gaily put it, 'Just a few minutes of cheerful chatter is all we want'. Ministers are prime targets for programme secretaries both inside and outside the church, for not only are they by definition speakers, they are also free during the daytime which is when most of these organizations meet.

The minister is expected to be at the centre of the church's organization and administration. This has to be carefully qualified. He is not expected by more than a few to be a dictator. Some like to cast him in the role of scapegoat for unpopular decisions. For almost everyone in the church, however, his is the opinion that matters. Whether or not they accept his judgement they rarely make a move until they know what it is. 'The minister says . . .' is usually sufficient justification when one church member defends a decision to another. Some ministers encourage a highly centralized, even autocratic, style of administration while others adopt the opposite strategy. This often causes confusion in churches where a minister with one style follows one with a different approach.

Naturally congregations expect that a minister will celebrate the sacrament of Holy Communion, though their reasons for this will vary from the theological to the sentimental. In my first appointment I had pastoral charge of over 300 members and was in every conceivable sense their minister, but because I was a probationer minister the Methodist authorities did not see fit to grant me a dispensation to conduct a communion service. After a few highly inconvenient attempts to draft in available supernumerary ministers to satisfy the requirements of the law, we gave up. I would announce at the start of the communion service that what followed would be strictly improper and that anyone who wished to withdraw was entirely free to do so. No one ever did. It was not the only instance of a local congregation having a good deal more common sense and theological acumen than the church establishment.

Most difficult to cope with was the church's expectation that the arrival of a new minister would herald the revival in the church's fortunes for which they had been looking so long in vain. Hope triumphs over experience and no matter how often they have been disappointed there remains the conviction in the minds of the congregation that it really will be the angel Gabriel next time. It is hard for a young minister not to be flattered by this and indeed to believe it, particularly if during his first month people's natural curiosity about a newcomer leads to larger congregations. He listens too eagerly to criticisms of his predecessor, forgetting that in time his own failings will be added to the oral tradition. He may not recognize that flattery is being used by one section of the church as a device to put him at the head of their struggle with another section. When the hoped-for revival does not take place the resulting disappointment and resentment can be very painful indeed.

If there are inconsistencies in the church's expectations of a minister, they are nothing compared with those of the community as a whole. Communities vary greatly and the expectations of village societies are very different from those in the suburbs and different again from those in new towns or in inner city areas. What follows therefore is especially personal and may not correspond to the experience of other ministers.

When a new minister arrives, certain expectations are already present in society and others are quickly created in the light of the minister's own special gifts and interests. In generally he is expected to be accessible. This is more a quality of his personality than of his diary. I soon noticed that if I walked into the shopping area wearing my clerical collar and greeted people, strangers or not, they would respond in a similar manner. When I repeated the procedure wearing a collar and tie the response usually suggested that I was someone who ought to be locked up. The minister is expected to set impeccable standards in his personal and family life. Even those who have no commitment or loyalty to the church often feel shock and pain when a minister is found guilty of some serious misdemeanour. Though it is trivial I perhaps ought to mention the widespread but inexplicable expectation that a minister will be seriously upset by bad language. While it is true that few of us use it, I have always felt that my stamina was being called in question when an apology for swearing is directed at me alone.

Then there are the expectations which are easily aroused if the minister shows a particular interest or skill in any direction. Some ministers rapidly become known to the press and local radio station as good for instant comment on matters of the day. Some ministers take great care to master the intricacies of the welfare state in order to use its resources effectively in helping people. They find that people who are nervous of officialdom are glad of their help as inter-mediaries. Some ministers develop special skills in marriage guidance or other kinds of counselling, some have a gift for communicating with young people and so are in demand for school assemblies and Founders' Day services. These and other specialist skills the community is usually glad to use.

Reflecting on these early experiences of being a minister there seem to have been a number of pressures shaping my ministry in unhelpful ways, in the absence of a more adequate model of ministry towards which I might direct myself. Indeed not only did I lack a clear understanding of what a minister was, neither had I appreciated the ways in which society had changed since the days when many of the people whose examples I was trying to follow had exercised their ministries. To give a couple of simple illustrations; I remember trying to draw up a balanced weekday programme for the church which would involve the members in church activities on two or three nights each week in addition to any business meetings. I was thinking of the days when the church was not only at the centre of the community but provided much of its social life. Then again I had been taught that the basic pattern of a minister's life was study in the morning, visiting in the afternoon and meetings in the evening. Yet it was soon apparent that only a minority of the population were available to be visited in the afternoon and that this minority was getting smaller all the time. As for evening visiting, the television was rapidly becoming the most important home-based leisure activity, turning many living rooms into mini-cinemas. The significance of this for a visitor is that whereas many leisure activities can be interrupted and taken up again later, watching a television programme cannot. Hence an entirely new strategy was needed.

Of these unhelpful pressures I can perhaps single out the three most important.

First, there is the desire to be liked. Of all occupations, the ministry leaves a person free to determine the pattern of each day. Lacking a fixed timetable and having no employer looking over one's shoulder, a young minister very easily accepts his congregation's estimate of how well he is using his time. He forgets his Lord's warning, 'Woe unto you when all men speak well of you', and instead looks eagerly for signs that his people appreciate him. This pressure is particularly intense from a few members of his church who, because they contribute to the fund from which the minister is paid, are under the impression that they actually employ him. They forget that the offertory is dedicated to God each week and not to the circuit stewards. Some of them will peer at the minister's diary while he is looking to see if he is free to accept a particular invitation. It was only later that I learned to fill in all the blanks with a sort of code, Family Fellowship standing for an evening out with my wife, Creche Commmittee for an evening in so that my wife could go out, Cultural Meeting for a visit to the cinema and so on.

Secondly, there is the feeling of deep personal resonsibility for every aspect of the life of the church. This means that every criticism of the church is taken by the minister as a criticism of himself whether or not it was so intended, and every proposal for action is regarded as a proposal for action by the minister. The result is a deep feeling of guilt over the decline of the institutional church and a sense of being overwhelmed by all that needs to be done.

Thirdly, his uncertainty about the nature and usefulness of his chosen profession leads a minister to try to make a contribution which can be understood and evaluated in secular terms. Thus some become involved in an aspect of the community's voluntary service programme and others become part-time teachers. Some are heavily committed to local political movements, or to broadcasting, or to community development, and some become in effect freelance entertainers appearing regularly at Rotary Clubs, Townswomen's Guilds, Darby and Joan Clubs and suchlike.

Some may want to resist my description of this last tendency as unhelpful. Let me explain more carefully. None of the activities I have listed are bad in themselves nor are they inconsistent with a minister's calling. They are appropriate not only to his leisure time but also to a segment of his working time. The problem lies in containing them and confining them to an ancillary place within a person's total ministry. When they give a minister a sense of identity he cannot find elsewhere, they may begin to occupy so much of his time that two serious questions are raised. First, it will be asked if it is right for the church to pay a full-time salary to a part-time worker. It is one thing for the church to see social work, broadcasting, etc., as part of its total mission, but another matter for it to present these sectors of society with a part-time worker free of charge without having made a conscious and deliberate decision to do so. Secondly, and more seriously, the question about what a minister is and whether he ought to feel a real sense of identity even without secular recognition is allowed to go by default. I was invited to speak to one of our theological colleges about the work of a circuit minister. During question time one of the students said that his great fear was that he seemed to be about to leave college a second-rate social worker, a second-rate teacher, a second-rate psychologist and a second-rate scholar. He felt condemned to spend his life being the jack of all trades and the master of none. I replied to the effect that he was right to fear this second-class status but that the answer was to spend one's life becoming a first-rate minister. This reply did not seem to be well received. It sounded facile and for that I blame myself. I was not able on that occasion to spell out what I meant. The aim of the next section will be to remedy this defect.

Towards a Contemporary Model of the Ministry
Humanly speaking two things sustained me through the period of confusion about the nature of the ministry. It will be seen that I have only providence to thank for this as they involve no special qualifications on my part. Some of my contemporaries, far more gifted and able men than myself, have come to the conclusion that there is no longer any role for the ministry and have left it. They are a real loss to the church, though I do not doubt they are still serving Christ and his kingdom with great effectiveness. That I did not follow them I attribute to two things above all else.

The first is the evidence that a minister is needed. He may be needed by the wrong people for the wrong reasons but there is no question that he is needed. When ministers get together to have a grumble about their problems I have never heard one say that he sits twiddling his thumbs and wondering what on earth to do. On the contrary all the conversation is about pressure and stress. I think all ministers would say that their difficulties over time are due to not having enough of it rather than having too much. Demands on a ministers time crowd in on him every day.

The second is the unashamedly subjective reason that I actually enjoy being a minister and find the task of becoming a better minister worth struggling with, however daunting the odds against me. I find it hard to say why I enjoy being a minister without giving the impression that a minister's job is in some way more important than any other—the last thing I want to do. I suppose the real reason is only a slight refinement of the very unworthy motive I had at the beginning in the school chapel. The most important thing in the world to me is the advancement of the Kingdom of God. The way in which I feel happiest to share in this advancement is as a minister. I am at the heart of things and of the things that matter most. It seems infinitely preferable to be a very minor ineffective part of the most important movement in the world than to be at the head of a movement of no consequence. Given the choice between doing badly something of great worth and becoming an expert at something trivial I must choose the former. I understand why Marxists are glad to die for the Revolution though they have no hope of resurrection. They have put their shoulders to the wheel of destiny. I happen to believe that the revolutionary purposes of God are even more significant than the creation of a new economic order (though they certainly include this) and that to think only in terms of the physical universe and our brief sojourn in it is to limit unnecessarily the context in which we see ourselves. To be a part of God's work—even the smallest possible part—is more than sufficient reason for me to be a minister.

However it cannot rest there. Two reasons for staying in the ministry do not begin to say what a minister is, let alone what he ought to be. I console myself by thinking that all theology is really the rationalizing of what we experience and that at least I can claim the virtue of doing this openly.

I find I am bound to think of a minister from the point of view of what he does rather than what he is. In a sense what he *is* is crucial for he is a minister because he has been ordained and recognized by the church. Thinking along these lines, however, only takes me in a circle. Question: What is a minister? Answer: Someone ordained by the church. Question: Then what is someone ordained by the church? Answer: A minister. So let me stick to what he does. In the course of doing what a minister does there will be occasions when people accord to him a certain status which will assist the work of the Kingdom. So be it. But fundamental are the things he does. Five of these are specially important and the combination of the five is even more important than the individual functions.

The source of these five is the Bible and my experience of the church. My understanding of the Bible tests my experience and my experience modifies my understanding. In an absolute sense the minister and the church do not need each other; many churches thrive without an ordained minister and some ministers pioneer outside the church. In general, however, minister and church depend on each other, drawing meaning, identity and support one from the other. I have mentioned some of the unhelpful aspects of the church's expectations of its minister. I want also to say that it is only possible to gain any idea of what a minister should be through the experience of being a minister to people, through discovering and meeting their real needs and being helped by them to discover one's own deepest needs. My relationship with the church is like two parts of a space ship trying to dock in outer space. There is a way we fit together but it is not easy to find it. We try from this angle and that and sometimes it takes a long time but we persevere because we know that we need to be together and that on our own we are not what we were intended to be. Here then are the five parts of the model.

1. *A minister is a pastor.* The most frequent biblical metaphor for pastor is shepherd and though this word can have a remote and sentimental ring for twentieth-century city dwellers its meaning is not beyond us. People need to feel cared for and to know that somebody is concerned about them. There are occasions when they need to speak to someone in absolute confidence. Those who find their relationships difficult may be helped by another's unhesitating acceptance. A minister is a caring and an accepting person. He may or may not care about humanity but he must care for

people. He may feel the need to acquire certain skills in order to express his care more effectively but the care can go a long way without skills whereas the skill is worthless without the care. In this a minister differs from a doctor, though the two professions are often regarded similarly. A doctor may benefit his patients even in the absence of personal concern, though of course concern will make him an even better doctor. A minister without concern is quite simply in the wrong job.

2. *A minister is a prophet.* A prophet is God's spokesman. He interprets the Spirit of God in the circumstances of the present day. He can only claim to speak with authority if his own devotional life maintains a close relationship with God and an openness to his Spirit. Nevertheless, he must speak because God needs his voice. God does not address mankind through some celestial tannoy. God needs the words of his prophets.

3. *A minister is a creator of communities.* People need communities to live in and the Christian gospel is about the quality of communities. The local church needs to become a healing and creative community and the minister's role in this will be crucial. He has to exercise this role with great care lest he inhibit the development of the whole people of God who form the church. His task is to help the church receive the gifts of all its members. The church must not be allowed to shelter behind its minister. Each member has received something from God with the intention that it should be shared so that the church community might be a source of healing and hope for society as a whole. The minister's creative role is to set people free for this.

4. *A minister is a theologian.* By this I mean one whose training and timetable gives him the opportunity to think about God and the ways in which his revelation in Jesus applies to people living today and preparing for tomorrow. Ignorance about the nature of God and the way he works is as serious in its consequences for the world as ignorance about any other aspect of our universe.

5. *A minister helps people to worship.* Without the experience of worship, awe, wonder, rapture, devotion and reverence, lives are impoverished. We need the experience of being turned away from ourselves and transported beyond

the here and now to catch a glimpse of eternity. Most people enjoy such experience without any help at least occasionally. One of the most important tasks of the church is to help people experience worship more frequently and more richly and to interpret worship so that it does not turn into self-indulgence. In the ordering of its worship the church gives its ministers special responsibility.

In the fivefold model I can see the outline of a person whose role is important if the world is to perceive and the church to embody the good news which is expressed in the birth, life, death and resurrection of Jesus. Much less importantly I see also the outline of someone I should like to become and consider it worth devoting my best gifts and my whole life to becoming.

Nevertheless, some will find it insufficient. Many of the elements that are often thought to be essential to the ministry are not there. These omissions are not accidental, but before moving on I will try to anticipate some of my critics.

'You haven't mentioned the sacraments.' The sacraments are central to the life of the church and vital to me personally but I cannot share the view of those who would confine the celebration of the Holy Communion to the ordained clergy. I cannot separate responsibility for the sacraments from a minister's general responsibility for worship. The creation of a priestly class within the church who alone could make the sacrament 'valid' took place towards the end of the first century AD. It represented a victory for the judaistic element in the early church who, having lost the crucial battle to Paul at the Council of Jerusalem, were determined that the ministry of the church should be modelled on the levitical priesthood in order to preserve its purity. The idea of a priestly class with unique functions within the church has no place in my thinking about the ministry.

'You haven't mentioned preaching.' I preferred to speak of the minister as a prophet rather than a preacher because there are more ways of speaking on behalf of God than preaching. A prophet may be a writer, for example, or a film director, or a cartoonist. I do regard preaching as important, believing that the conveying of great truths through the personality of the preacher can be a most powerful way of communicating the gospel.

'People do not want theologians or promoters of worship experiences. You condemn the minister to irrelevance.' There is certainly no desire for incomprehensible theologians or for the boring routine that passes for worship in many of our churches, but there are numerous signs of a need for people who can think clearly about life's most important themes and of the desire for experiences of transcendence.

'All the functions you list can be performed by lay people. We have lay theologians and lay pastors, in what way does your model distinguish a minister?' I would go further than this critic and say that all these functions must be performed by lay people if the church is to experience wholeness. One of the most unfortunate results of ministers' uncertainty about their role has been their claim of exclusive responsibility in certain areas in order to justify themselves. What distinguishes a minister (and the distinction is not absolute) is that he possesses a certain combination of gifts and functions. This can be illustrated by reference to other professions. If you ask what is special about a barrister apart from the fact that he is authorized to plead in certain courts you would find that his various qualifications, knowledge of the law, ability to speak, a quick mind, understanding of human nature, and so on, were all shared by other people and were not exclusive to the profession of barrister. What distinguishes a barrister is that in himself he combines a certain package of qualifications and it is the package that enables him to perform the task to which he has been appointed. So it is with a minister.

Tension and the Ministry
Everyone's life involves tension. Every Christian life involves special tensions, in particular the tension between the person as he is and the person he ought to be. A minister's life is subject to special tensions, however, which, while not exclusive to the ministry, need to be appreciated if the nature of the ministry today is to be properly understood.

I have already referred to the tension between the sort of minister I want to be and the minister the church and the community expect me to be. I may feel very deeply about the need for Christians to be involved in local and national politics and I may be strongly in sympathy with one of the main parties. At the same time I know that if my commitment to a particular party is too strong it may set up damaging tensions within the church, and that when I try to speak as a community leader on a matter of public concern I shall be thought to be making only a party political point. I may judge that the work of God will be facilitated if a particular church is allowed to close, but the congregation will want me to strive to keep it open. There will be some who expect me to visit them once a month and who will be loud in their praise or criticism. There are others whose diffidence or modesty means that the minister will have to seek them out and who will never say a word to anyone about whether they have been helped by his call or not. The temptation to pay special attention to the former group is very strong yet has to be resisted at all costs.

There is tension between being available and being available to those who need you most. It is tempting to give an impression of great industry, partly to offset the guilt feelings many ministers have about leisure, and partly for fear of being thought lazy by the congregation. At the same time I know that many of the people who need help most will never come near me if they think that I am busy. If they come we may need plenty of time before they can get to what they really wanted to say. So though I shall inevitably be rather busy I must give the impression of having nothing to do that will not wait until tomorrow. Of course there are some who, given half a chance, would gladly occupy all a minister's time, and I shall have to recognize them and keep them at arm's length lest they suffocate me.

There is tension between the values of the 'career' of minister and the career values of everyone else. In almost every job or profession people advance through training and experience to positions of greater responsibility, significance and reward. In contrast, a minister begins at the position of greatest responsibility, that is of being a pastor to people. In many denominations the real value of his stipend remains unchanged throughout his ministry, and any change in the nature of his appointment will lead to a dilution of the basic work of the ministry by a higher proportion of church administration. That there is a need for ministers to work 'behind the front lines' is not in doubt. We need strategists, educators, pastors to the pastors, and so on, but we should not confuse a greater area of responsibility with a greater degree of responsibility. Within hours of taking up my first appointment as a minister I was in the home of an elderly lady whose husband had been drowned in a boating accident a few days previously. I have never at any time in my ministry since been in a more important or responsible position than that. This particular tension is made worse by the fact that most lay people assume that the career values of the ministry are the same as their own and so speak about 'promotion' to superintendent, bishop, connexional secretary, etc.

There is tension between the work of a minister and his home and family life. The ministry is not alone in this but for a number of reasons the work of the church flows readily into the home, sometimes threatening to drown it. His lack of fixed hours of duty, the ownership of his home by the church, the presence of a study or office within his home, and the fact that often his wife and family belong to the church, all tend to blur the normal distinctions between a minister's work and his private life. The church has expectations too of the minister's wife which are not experienced by other wives, nor indeed by the husbands of women ministers.

There are tensions between freedom and discipline. Because a minister is more free than anyone else who works for a living, to plan his own time and determine his own priorities, he seems to be most likely to become a helpless victim of pressures outside his control. He becomes afraid of the blank spaces in his diary, regarding them as a sign of inactivity. He feels guilty about spending a whole morning reading a book. He finds it hard to say no to this or that invitation when he feels people expect him to say yes. He does not like spending Tuesday morning in the garden because he imagines that passers-by are thinking that their husbands had to be at the factory or office by nine o'clock. He realizes in a way that they will clock off at half past four while he will be at a meeting till ten o'clock and then in his study till past midnight, but this fails to stop him feeling uneasy about the gardening.

These tensions are never resolved; the best a minister can do is to find a way of living with them. Those who do this most successfully are those who discover inner resources for their work. This will not make them indifferent to the nature of the church or their society for they will always be learning from them, nor will they disregard the ministerial models of the past for there is still much to be learned from them. They will put their deepest roots down elsewhere however, in their own model of a minister derived from their understanding of what God wants from his people and his church, and from this they will draw the richest nourishment. I have offered my model in the hope that it will help others to discover theirs.

Lessons for the Future

There are certain things which, if I had understood them at the outset of my ministry might have spared me and the church some of our pain.

(a) *The changing nature of the community.* Models of ministry from a previous age need to be treated with the utmost caution. Urbanization, the advent of television, the appearance of the nuclear family, the rising living standards of working people, new opportunities for leisure, have all changed our society beyond recognition. If the minister is not a central figure in the community any more it is not because his place has been usurped. It is because there are no communities in the traditional sense, apart from in rural villages, and hence no community leaders in the traditional style.

(b) *The proper relationship of the minister to his church.* He is not the one who makes things happen. At best he is the one who enables things to happen.

(c) *The right relationship between the various parts of the church's structure.* The church must resist all tendencies to acquire a hierarchy or pyramid structure after the pattern of secular institutions. These give the impression that power and significance increase as one ascends the pyramid. It cannot be emphasized too strongly that there is no more significant job in the church that on the frontier which is the local church or parish. This is where people come under the influence of the gospel. The only justification for any other part of the church's organization is that it enables the local church to be more truly and effectively the body of Christ.

(d) *The essential loneliness of the minister.* More perhaps than in any other job a minister depends on being able to discover what it is that God is saying to him. He has no objective criteria against which to measure his performance. He must not simply fit into the church and community in case they should both be the wrong shape. No one can prescribe a timetable because no one can anticipate what needs and opportunities each day will bring. This sense of divine uncertainty is for many ministers one of the great attractions of their work. Nevertheless, it imposes a burden which can never be wholly shared. The support of those closest to him, be they family or colleagues, is invaluable for a minister, but he can never be wholly shielded from the sense of being naked and exposed with no stronger protection than his understanding of what it is to belong to Christ and to serve him in the world. As this understanding does not amount to very much he spends his life trying to make it more, being a minister and becoming one at the same time, being shaped by a hundred influences yet trying to ensure that most of all he is affected by the Spirit of God. He is called to share with others what he has only imperfectly received for himself, a sense of vocation and the experience of living in the power of love. His greatest joy lies in the discovery that the more he gives the more he receives. So minister and people help each other, and, though often it is no more than two bewildered travellers sharing fragments of a torn map, they grow together towards the wholeness which is Christ.

Postscript

Since writing all that has gone before, news has come that my church wishes me to leave the circuit appointment where I now am and to move to an appointment where my responsibilities will be national rather than local. Making the right response to this has been one of the hardest decisions of my life. If I am loyal to the church I must go, but I am also a human being and still too much of a sinner to find it easy to leave the church's front line where I want to be and where I believe the really important work is done. Is it possible to be a minister without having a congregation to minister to? or is it possible to discover a community in the whole church? Can I ever criticize the leadership of the church if I decline the invitation to become part of that leadership? No, to deny myself that would be too much to bear! Of course there must be those whose job is to supply the ammunition to the front-line troops, to care for the wounded, and to encourage and direct reinforcements to the hard pressed. But will it be as satisfying as talking to a teenager about the meaning of discipleship or to a father about the meaning of baptism?—and does it matter if it is not? We shall see. Rather more worrying—will I be able to resist the pressures to become an ecclesiastical bureaucrat, hemmed in by the machinery of church administration, increasingly isolated from the real world? Will they believe me, those front-line troops of the future, when I tell them from my comfortable London office that theirs is the most important job of all, or will they regard me as a patronizing old fool who has opted out? I do not think I could bear that.

You see—already I am beginning to worry about what people think of me, just like the day I left theological college. Is there no end to the struggle to do the right thing because it is the right thing? There is no end in sight. Then is it worth the struggle? It is worth it, and that is one of the few things of which I have not the slightest doubt.

3

From Priesthood to Ministry

Peter Hebblethwaite

Peter Hebblethwaite joined the Jesuits in 1948 at the age of seventeen. He studied in France and at Oxford, and was ordained in 1963. He was Editor of the *Month* from 1967 to 1973. He parted amicably with the Jesuits in 1974. He has subsequently been a freelance writer and broadcaster and, from 1976, Lecturer in French at Wadham College, Oxford.

Most recent books: *The Runaway Church* (Collins 1976 and paperback 1978); *Christian-Marxist Dialogue and Beyond* (Darton, Longman and Todd 1977); and *The Year of Three Popes* (Collins 1978).

In the official parlance of the Roman Catholic Church, to which I loyally belong, I am a 'laicized priest'. Since January 1974 I have ceased to exercise any sacramental ministry. I have never previously written about this experience, and never intended to, for the simple reason that I did not think that my individual case was significant for a wider public. I have not changed my mind: but at the same time the opportunity to think on paper about some aspects of the ministry today was too tempting to resist. We are at an ecumenical turning point. Disparate traditions are converging through a return to the biblical sources.

I am, then, an 'ex-priest'. Those who belong to Christian Churches which reject or are suspicious of the language of 'priesthood' may need some explanation of what this means. In its simplest terms, and as codified by the sixteenth-century Council of Trent, Catholic teaching stated that a man (and only a man) entered the priesthood by the sacrament of ordination which empowered him to celebrate the Eucharist and to 'forgive sins'. It ushered him into a state of life which was irrevocable, celibate and 'different in essence' from the lay state. Like confirmation, ordination conferred a *sphragis* or seal of the Holy Spirit (usually called 'character') which marked him out in this world and the next.

But if that is what a priest is in Roman Catholic teaching, it would seem impossible to be an 'ex-priest'. The character or seal cannot be effaced. The ontological status can never be lost. And the sacramental powers can never be removed. It is, then, impossible in the strict sense to be an 'ex-priest'. What happens to those who are popularly called 'ex-priests' is that they receive from the appropriate channels a 'dispensation' from their priestly vows and permission to marry. But this dispensation does not abolish their priesthood: rather it puts the priesthood, so to speak, in the deep freezer. Or to use a less ghoulish metaphor, this treasure is locked up inside me, never more to be called upon in ordinary circumstances. But it remains and in case of grave emergency or dire spiritual need—the street accident or the concentration camp—it could be 'revived'.

All the vocabulary, popular and official, is misleading. To be laicized sounds like being thrust back into the ranks from which one came, and of course the laicized priest will to all outward appearances behave like a layman. But that does not alter the fact that his 'suspended' priesthood 'perdures' (another technical term from Trent). There is, by the way, no rite to accompany the process of laicization: it is not like being stripped of one's rank in the army. One receives a letter, sometimes after agonizing delays, from the appropriate Roman office.

As a laicized priest, I have received many confidences from other priests who wished to resign from the ministry. They think they will find in me a sympathetic ear, and I hope I have not disappointed them. I would like, first of all, to reflect on their experience, their *trauma*, before seeking in Vatican II the basis of a renewed vision of the ministry which could be of interest for all Christians. There is a subterranean link between the two sections: for if the first part of this chapter will be concerned with some of the effects of Tridentine theology, the second part will strive to show how that theology has been to some extent dismantled or at least set in a different context.

There are a number of reasons why a man who resigns from the priesthood will be marked for life, some theological, some sociological, and some in between. The first reason is that he was seen by Catholics essentially as a 'sacred' person in a higher state of life. He mediated God. No higher vocation could be conceived, and his parents and relations would gather for his ordination which was, according to the cliché, 'the greatest day in his life'. As a sign of his sacredness he was 'set apart', perhaps from his earliest days in a seminary, but certainly later on by his life-style, his readiness to be moved about by bishop or religious superior, and his celibacy. Because of his sacred status, he could get away with much. Catholics would be generous, understanding, forgiving if need be. 'It's the office and not the man who counts', they used to say, and Graham Greene in *The Power and the Glory* exploited the paradox of the sinner who could nevertheless remain a vehicle of grace.

The paradox could sometimes tip over into absurdity. Was it better to be a bad priest than an ex-priest? Yes, said a whole tradition which emphasized his sacred status. It followed that to break with the priesthood was *tabu*.

The same points can be put in sociological language. The sacred status of the priest assigned him a 'role' in the community of the Church. This was signified by distinctive dress. Dress is an immediate instance of 'non-verbal communication' and it points to a given role in society. By insisting on strict clerical dress, ecclesiastical conservatives like the late Cardinal Heenan have correctly judged that dress defines a role better than anything else, and that a man who changes his dress may shortly change his conception of his role. For a time, the polo-necked sweater was all the rage, which led someone to speak of 'apostles disguised as fishermen'. But the man who puts on a tie ceases to be quite so different from the laity and quite so amenable to authority.

There is a further reason why leaving the priesthood is traumatic. The priesthood is a role in a 'total institution', one that encompasses every aspect of life, both material and spiritual. The priest has a vocation, and therefore he is never off-duty. There is no moment in the day, no time in his life, when he can doff his priesthood. In retreats and other spiritual exercises he is exhorted never to forget that he is a priest, 'to become like that which he handles', and above all to become a priest *interiorly* so to speak. [1] Moreover his thoughts should increasingly be the thoughts of the Church. Of course he is urged to assimilate them personally but he does not forget that he takes his place in a long line of official witnesses.

It is difficult to conceive of a more 'total institution'. And the more total the institution, the greater the wrench that

[1] For that reason I find the following comment of Dr Alec Vidler incomprehensible. In retirement at Rye he has an ex-directory number: 'This precaution has saved me . . . from being rung up on Saturday evenings by vicars' wives, asking me to take their husband's duty on the morrow as he has an incipient cold' (*Scenes from a Clerical Life*, Collins. 1977).

accompanies departure. The removal, the sudden removal, of the supportive milieu can be very disturbing. All the props on which one traditionally relied have been knocked away. In particular, the esteem of the peer-group, in this instance fellow priests, if it does not evaporate altogether, remains a matter of guesswork. He does not know in advance what other priests will think of the step he is taking. With hindsight I have noted five characteristic responses. (1) Condemnation: he has let down or betrayed the Church. (2) Awkwardness: he poses a problem that no one wants to face. (3) Compassion: it is assumed, no doubt correctly, that he must be undergoing considerable strain, though by the time of the actual decision, much of the tension begins to depart. (4) Acceptance: he has done nothing very strange. (5) Admiration: he has behaved courageously in preferring integrity, often about celibacy, to uneasy or unworthy compromises. 2–4 are the commonest responses, from clergy and laity. But the would-be ex-priest does not know that.

It is not easy to make a break with a 'total institution'. That is why one sometimes has the distressing phenomenon of priests who turn against and denounce what they once loved. Many ex-priests feel impelled to produce an *apologia* for their step which relieves a psychological need as much as it illumines their situation. Though they are ostensibly writing about the iniquities of the Church and the Roman Curia, a rich vein, they are really writing about themselves and their disappointed hopes. That may seem a patronizing judgement, but nothing else can explain the violence of early hasty statements which are afterwards regretted. They remain and poison the atmosphere.

The tendency to disparage the Church is unwittingly encouraged by delays in the Roman bureaucracy. One of the melancholy tasks of anyone wishing to resign from the priesthood is to write a brief spiritual autobiography giving the reasons for his decision. I have heard that such documents are destroyed once they have been considered, which is good for the individuals but bad for future historians. In 1971 there appeared a rescript or letter to bishops and religious superiors which gave advice on how to apply for a dispensation. Some applicants were not producing sound reasons. It was not enough, for example, to mention the mere desire to get married, nor was it any use attempting a civil marriage, still less hopefully fixing the date of a religious ceremony. What the Sacred Congregation most wanted to know was that there had been a long history of conflict with authorities and deep difficulties with faith. These were regarded as better grounds than love. It is clear that if the 'right' answers are given, analysis will than show that the Church is simply releasing its trouble-makers and those who were in any case losing their faith. Q.E.D. It will also be possible to claim that the problem of priestly identity has little to do with obligatory celibacy.

In my experience, the evidence points the other way. It is not usually dissatisfaction with the ministry as such which comes first, but dissatisfaction with celibacy as an indispensable condition of the ministry. True 'falling in love' may be a symptom indicating that something is wrong in the ministry. But such an explanation is not required: to fall in love all that is needed is to belong to the human race. In any event, once a man has resigned from the ministry, he is likely to marry, and marry quickly and perhaps unwisely. The reason is obvious. To be suddenly alone and without a supportive milieu is deeply distressing, so the fresh ex-priest seeks to remedy the situation. I would not, however, go so far as Philip Berrigan who wrote: 'Most priests marry for therapeutic reasons—they seek a wife as others seek a psychiatrist' (*Prison Journals of a Priest Revolutionary,* Ballantine Books, New York, 1971). There is certainly extra pressure on the married priest and his wife. He knows that there are some of his former colleagues who take a cynical view and are prepared to gloat over failure. I cannot count the number of times I have heard it reported, with total inaccuracy, that the marriage of X, a well-known theologian, was on the point of breaking up. Such unworthy *Schadenfreude* is an attempt to seek consolation on the part of those who remain in the trenches: the supposed failure of the marriage would prove that the ex-priest had made a mistake.

Having said that much, it is only fair to add that the only thing which ex-priests have in common is that they are ex-priests. Otherwise they have an individual story to tell, and the notion of gathering them together in groups to discuss their situation and compare their wives is distasteful: it is an instance of post-clerical clericalism. Nor can one generalize

65

about the work they go on to do. Most of them are used to working long but somewhat vague hours; and there are few jobs in which such a work-style can be continued. Some slip easily into teaching, and English academic life has been enriched by a number of ex-priests. But others, without special qualifications, have a miserable time and end up in dead-end jobs which sap the spirit. In America it is alleged that ex-priests make excellent insurance salesmen, perhaps because they were previously engaged in selling a form of celestial insurance.

Their present relationship to the Church is the principal grounds for distinguishing between them. There are those who abandon the Church and the priesthood simultaneously, either quietly or fortissimo. They want no more to do with the Church. They have despaired, they say, of Church reform. She is unfaithful to the message she preaches. But this is rare. A commoner experience is that a man becomes weary of preaching what he has come to consider as an ethereal message and concentrates instead on social and political commitment. When this happens, we have a practical instance of 'secularization'. In the British Isles this usually leads into counselling or social work; in Latin countries to left-wing political action (*communautés de base* are welcoming); and in Latin America it can lead straight into revolutionary commitment. Ex-bishop Podesta of the Argentine has been obliged to flee his country for fear of right-wing assassins.

Other ex-priests have a different theory and a different self-understanding. The Church as we know it is doomed, they explain, and they are the prophets and heralds of the new Church which will be built up from the grass roots. They find sympathetic small groups which are ready to accept their message and their ministry. Much excitement is generated. I find this position presumptuous but not utterly nonsensical. If at some future date Rome were to authorize the ordination of married men to the priesthood, it would then be difficult to exclude those priests who have married and want to return. This, indeed, is one of the reasons for the extreme hesitation in the ordination of married men. Those who have advocated it have usually done so on the grounds of pastoral need and the shortage of priests; but if, with the Canadian Bishops, one goes further and says that it is a Good Thing and that the ordination of married men would actually enrich the priesthood by bringing a wealth of fresh experience, then the continued exclusion of 'priests who had married' would be more difficult to justify.

But that day seems far off in the present climate. There is some evidence that ex-priests are discrimated against. In Italy the Concordat makes it difficult for them to find work of any kind, and they are not allowed to teach even non-religious subjects. The young must be preserved at all costs from their noxious influence. Elsewhere the ban is usually limited to teaching theology. A new feature is that many theology professors today have contracts with secular universities which means that they cannot be dismissed from their posts simply because they resign from the priesthood; yet Roman congregations insist that they be removed. One reason a lecturer in, say, Old Testament studies is likely to insist on maintaining his contract is that there are anyway few posts available for which he would be suited, and dismissal would mean not only financial embarrassment but probably the complete abandonment of his specialized studies for which there is no market outside theological institutions. But even if he cannot legally be forced to leave, pressure will be put upon him to resign 'voluntarily'. [2]

I suppose that there is a certain logic in saying that future priests ought not to be taught by ex-priests: after all, they have devalued the currency. But in Roman minds there is a further assumption that there must be something wrong with a man's theological thinking if he has been led to abandon the priesthood. The assumption may be justified in some cases, but it by no means follows logically, unless one is going to make the further assumption that there is something intrinsically wicked and disgraceful in resigning from the priesthood. Deep down, one suspects that this remains the official presupposition. It is understandable enough, because to question it radically might make leaving the priesthood too attractive

---

[2] They order these things differently in Holland. At present there are over twenty married priests teaching in the five theological institutes. This contravention of Roman regulations is justified by the Dutch on the casuistic grounds that these appointments were made before the Roman regulations were published. Meanwhile, 'a dialogue is going on'.

or too easy. The slight air of discouragement helps to keep the troops in order and not break ranks. It is essential that one has *something to lose*. There is nothing surprising about this or particularly shocking: it is the way institutions respond to the threat of disintegration.

However, outside Rome, attitudes have changed and are still changing. My own experience has been extremely positive. Once the initial shock-waves had receded and after I had made it clear that I was in no way abandoning the Church, the way was open for a continuation of my previous ministry. I had been a religious journalist (what the French call distressingly an *informateur religieux*); I continued to be a religious informer. The friendship of many priests and some bishops survived the changed condition, and I have continued to serve, perhaps by oversight, on official Church bodies such as the Secretariat for Non-believers. Even Cardinal Heenan, whom I had gravely abused, took me aside at a conference and held my hand fondly. True, he was ticking me off for an incautious phrase, but at least he did not try to convert me. Cardinal Hume has been all Benedictine *pax*. After an initial journey through various *noms de guerre*, I have been able to write freely in my own name in Catholic newspapers and journals throughout the world—except in *The Universe*, an exclusion which is more an honour than a reproach.

I am thus led to the following conclusion. Though one may speak, with all the reservations discussed above, of 'leaving the priesthood', one can never speak of 'leaving the ministry'. One can relinquish in practice and with regret those sacramental activities which are proper to the ordained ministry; but one can never abandon the ministry itself since this is something in which all Christians participate. I continue to meet people and to lecture and to write: the ministry of the word and the ministry of reconciliation have not ceased. Obviously if one regards ex-priests as so many Judases—an unfortunate phrase let slip by Pope Paul one Maundy Thursday—then they cannot be expected to contribute anything further to the life of the Church. But if they are regarded as fellow-Christians who have exchanged one role in the Church for another, then they will have a contribution to make. I can envisage, without advocating, a general amnesty at some future date.

From Priesthood to Ministry

In the last paragraph I have deliberately started to speak of ministry rather than priesthood. This is not a stratagem for counting myself in, but a transition to the second part of this chapter. Moreover, this switch of vocabulary echoes the movement which has actually taken place in the Roman Catholic Church since Vatican Council II ended in 1965. Whereas the Council itself used the rather odd expression, 'the ministerial priesthood' (as though there could be a priesthood that were not ministerial), by the 1971 Roman Synod adjective and noun had changed places and the Synod spoke more happily of 'the priestly ministry'. This is more than a semantic quibble. It means that we must think first of the *ministry* and only later of the *priestly* ministry.

Let me illustrate this change of emphasis from the liturgy. *Lex orandi, lex credendi* is still a good maxim. In the Universal Prayer of Good Friday, the first invitation to prayer speaks of the *special ministry* of priests and bishops. But if the ministry of priests and bishops is a *special ministry*, this idea makes sense only against a background in which it is assumed that everyone in the Church shares in a *general* ministry. Against this backcloth, one can discern the special ministry. Priesthood, then, becomes a special case of ministry: it does not have a monopoly of ministry. And just as access to the special ministry in the Church is by way of a sacrament (called ordination), so access to the general ministry of the Church is by way of a sacrament, or rather by the sacramental complex of baptism/confirmation.

One can say that ministry or *diakonia* is the most fundamental concept in the New Testament: it is the concrete form that the imitation of Christ takes. He came not to be ministered to, but to minister. The washing of the disciples' feet in St John's Gospel expresses Jesus' self-sacrificing service of the brethren, and so interprets the meaning of his crucifixion. The imitation of Christ cannot mean that we should literally leap out of our skins and become first-century Jews: it can only mean that we assimilate, gradually but we hope increasingly, the mind of Christ so that his attitude of service becomes ours. From this point of view there is only one ministry in the Church, and we all share in it. The *whole* Church, by which I mean with St Augustine Christ conjoined by the Spirit to the community of believers, exercises a priestly ministry towards the world. There is one general ministry or *diakonia*.

Once this has been grasped, we can then go on to distinguish with the New Testament a great diversity of special ministries: and the diversity is rooted in the varied gifts of the Holy Spirit, showered upon the whole people, and expressed in practice through the variety of talents and temperaments. They are usually called *charismata*. 'To each is given the manifestation of the Spirit for the common good' (1 Cor. 12:17). And as 1 Peter puts it: 'As each has received a gift, employ it for one another' (1 Peter 4:10).

Provided they meet the criterion of building up the unity of the Church in love, the range of charismatic gifts and therefore of services is unlimited. There are gifts of leadership and gifts of healing. There are gifts of teaching and gifts of encouragement or consolation. I think that it helps if we see ourselves as engaged in this vast enterprise of the Spirit, in which all teach and all learn, because all are both apostles and disciples. And the forms of ministry should be seen very concretely: the mother teaching her child to pray, the student making sense of Christian faith for himself and others, the nurse who looks after the sick—these are just some examples of the way *diakonia* is working out. There is also what one might call an 'anonymous ministry', a ministry which has not yet been recognized but which is none the less real: it consists in the mutual help, support and enlightenment which we can bring to each other. Like M. Jourdain discovering that he had been speaking prose all his life without knowing it, so we may come to discover the ministry of everyday contacts. Even though it is true that the most fundamental ministry in St Paul is that of preaching, because it is in preaching that the reconciling word of God is proclaimed, this does not necessarily mean 'pulpit-preaching' in our modern sense; the word of healing and reconciliation can be spoken in the ordinary circumstances of human life.

But two qualifications must be added before we can attempt to apply New Testament ideas more fully to our present situation. I have so far written as though ministry in the Church depended entirely on charismatic gifts, and therefore welled up from below. But this is only half the picture. There is in the New Testament a concept of *office* as a stable state involving leadership in the community: this cannot be left out of account because it is part of the data. Alongside the charismatic, free-wheeling presentation of the ministry, in which distinctions between permanent ministries and occasional charisms seem fluid, one can find in the pastoral epistles of Titus and Timothy an account of ministry in which pastoral responsibility is handed on through the imposition of hands and the invocation of the Spirit. Ministry becomes organized; and it is this organized aspect of ministry which subsequent tradition has emphasized and developed, so much so that the charismatic conception of ministry disappeared from view. We are in a better position today to restore the balance.

The second qualification is that the New Testament avoids the language of 'priesthood' when it talks about ministry. It does, of course, speak of 'priesthood', but when this term is used, it is used exclusively of Christ, the unique high priest, the one in whom the levitical priesthood comes to an end. In Hebrews Christ is presented as entering the Holy of Holies once for all, irrevocably, unrepeatably. In the New Testament 'priestly' vocabulary either narrows down to focus on Christ alone, or broadens out to include the whole 'priestly people'. What is certain is that the notion of a separated priestly group or caste is done away with.

Theologians of the Catholic tradition thus have a problem. From about the third century sacerdotal language was reintroduced and applied to the ministry in the narrow sense. The Levites made a comeback. Ministry comes to be seen primarily as priesthood. And whereas talk of *ministry* stressed the unity with the rest of the Church, talk of *priesthood* stressed rather the separateness, the sacredness of the man who is set apart for holy things which the profane (here identified with the layman) cannot touch. The whole subsequent development of the priesthood with its celebacy, permanence, restriction to men only, flows from this changed conception. The deep roots of clericalism lie here. This is the point at which the 'priesthood of all the faithful' began to be relegated into the limbo of forgotten notions.

The 'Protestant' answer to this problem has generally been that the Church departed from its primitive tradition, and that it illegitimately fell back into Jewish habits of thought. The process was natural but misguided: the Church reinvented priesthood and sacrifice, and thus derogated from the unique priesthood and unique sacrifice of Christ. The most consistent and logical remedy for the situation is found in the Presbyterian tradition, which takes the priesthood of all the faithful seriously. And in this tradition, ministry is seen essentially as ministry of the word.

There is, however, an alternative and more 'Catholic' answer to this problem. It is the one adopted by the Anglican/Roman Catholic joint statement on the ministry. The reintroduction of Jewish vocabulary and concepts, says this theory, was not the result of judaizing tendencies, and the Old Testament priesthood has indeed come to an end. But the minister is seen as imitating Christ at the Last Supper. When he presides at the *synaxis* or eucharist he is likened to Christ at the Last Supper: there is evidence for this in iconography and in the works of Clement and Chrysostom. Thus the minister of the Eucharist may be called 'priest' by analogy with Christ, and this is a real analogy of participation. He may appropriately be called 'priest' because he does what Christ does, and because he makes present now the sacrifice of Christ which can be neither repeated nor added to.

This view, then, does not derogate from Christ's unique work, but it establishes an intimate link between the minister and Christ, and justifies language about the priest as *alter Christus*, 'another Christ', which has been the basis of priestly spirituality ever since. The celebration of the Eucharist is the central, and defining, task of the priest; just as it is the celebration of the Eucharist which is the central, and defining, event in the Church, *Ubi Eucharistia, ibi ecclesia:* where the Eucharist is, there also is the Church. The Church is unique among human groups in that it has a rite which expresses its nature, confirms it in its tasks, builds up its unity, and sends it off on its mission.

Manifestly, one can defend the need for a eucharistic *ministry* in the Church, but wonder whether it also implies permanent eucharistic *ministers*. This function is certainly necessary, but does it have to be tied to a permanent state of life in the Church? In other words: is a man (or a woman) a minister of the Eucharist only in the act of presiding at the Eucharist, after which they return to the body of the priestly people? Or does being a minister of the Eucharist carry with it an ontological status, a whole lifestyle and a degree of life-long commitment which mark off such ministers from the rest of the faithful? The Orthodox, Catholic and Anglican traditions give the second answer. Ordination can only be conferred once, and it is irrevocable. Catholics, we have already seen, used to speak of the 'character' or seal of the Spirit. The Anglican/Roman Catholic statement on ministry manages to make the same point while studiously avoiding the language of character. 'Their ministry', it says, 'is not an extension of the common Christian priesthood but belongs to another realm of the gifts of the Spirit' (Canterbury, 1973, No. 13).

So the eucharistic ministry sets up a state of life in the Church called priesthood. Does this mean, therefore, that we have not advanced beyond the Council of Trent which hardened these ideas in the polemical Counter-reformation situation? Yes and no. Trent simply rationalized a situation which existed: priests abounded, and in Europe their missionary impulse had given way to a holding operation. The one priestly activity common to all was the celebration of the Eucharist. But the Mass was only rarely a true eucharistic assembly. Many priests celebrated Mass alone, or with just a server present. One of the reasons for Luther's attack on the priesthood was their lack of any serious occupation; if they do not preach, he held, they are not true priests. Trent responded by under-valuing the preaching of the Word and placing the essence of the priesthood in the fact that certain men were enabled or empowered to celebrate Mass. This became the essential difference between priesthood and laity. One should note that here the priest is not defined in relation to the community which he exists to serve, but as one possessed of special powers. Sociological factors then supervened to make the priest a separated, sacred person, with all the consequences described in the first part of this chapter.

Vatican II, however, was not content with this inherited situation. It modified Trent in three important ways.[3] First, it revived the idea of 'the priesthood of all the faithful' and saw the priestly ministry against the background of the

[3] For a fuller treatment of the points made in this paragraph, cf. my book, *The Runaway Church*, Collins, 1975, chap. 4.

charismatic gifts of all the faithful. Secondly, it saw the priest's ministry not in isolation but in relation to the community he is there to serve: thus in principle the minister/people conflict is overcome, since the minister is not set 'over against' the people but is rather seen as their representative (cf. Romans 12:1). Thirdly, Vatican II re-established a balance between the eucharistic, sacramental role of the priest and his task as preacher of the Word: Word and Sacrament were seen as buttressing, as calling for each other.

None of this, admittedly, is enough completely to subvert Trent or to lead us to reject the idea of the 'priestly ministry' as a permanent state. Priesthood is not yet regarded as a function rather than a state in the Roman Catholic Church. Nevertheless, we can build on the emphases of Vatican II to raise the following questions.

(1) The ordination of married men is no longer a difficulty. It has never, in fact, been a theoretical difficulty since the example of the early Church as well as the Oriental Churches in communion with Rome proved that priesthood and marriage were not mutually exclusive. But it has been a psychological difficulty, so long as the priest was separated from the community, and based his spirituality on the arduous merits of separation. If on the contrary one wishes to stress his insertion in the community then sharing in the ordinary lot of humanity becomes an advantage rather than a handicap. Thus the argument in favour of the ordination of married men would not be based on the shortage of unmarried priests and rather on the value to the whole Church which would flow from their ordination. It would also help to clear up the nagging suspicion that the requirement of celibacy is based on hostility to sexuality, and at the same time make celibacy stand out as a freely chosen state which presupposes a special gift or charism. There seems to be some inconsistency in turning what is acknowledged to be a charism into a universal obligation.

The argument is sometimes used that to ordain married men would have the most devastating effects among the ranks of the existing celibate clergy, and that they would all rush off and get married or at least feel resentful at having missed out. If there is anything in this argument, which comes in the main from conservatives, it would betray a lamentable judgement on the present celibate clergy, who would be revealed at best as reluctant celibates.

(2) A pastoral 'team' exercising diversified ministries could become the pattern for the future. It could include catechists, social workers, psychiatrists, musicians for the liturgy, poets and even those who possess the special charism of financial wizardry. This 'model' already is beginning to exist in some places. The notion of a parish priest as a one-man pastoral band is clearly unworkable. Whether these other ministries require a special rite of ordination may be doubted: the working out of the sacrament of confirmation might be considered a sufficient general 'deputation' for tasks which can be specified as needs arise and talents are revealed. This seems to be more important than asking, as the English Roman Catholic Bishops did at their 1976 Low Week meeting, whether the ministries of acolyte and reader should be 'examined afresh' (*Infoform,* 8 May 1976). The bishops rightly foresaw trouble if such proposed ministries were to be confined to men. Rather than try to plan new ministries on the drawing-board, it seems better to look at what is actually happening and to encourage promising developments. We have already seen how the revival of the diaconate has tended to produce clericalized laymen to plug sacerdotal gaps rather than any real penetration into the secular world of work.

(3) New ministries are emerging, and new forms of leadership. This can happen through the charismatic movement, or through the more politically oriented *communautés de base* which are mushrooming in Latin America and elsewhere, or through the growing importance of catechists as builders of the community in Africa. That such groups should have to wait for the arrival of an ordained priest before they can celebrate the Eucharist seems anomalous, if it be true that it is the Eucharist which creates the Church. *Sacramenta propter homines:* the sacraments are for people, is one of the most ancient theological maxims. We are in danger of relapsing into a religion of the word or of action, and thus losing our grip on the central mystery of salvation which is proclaimed in the Eucharist. It would make sociological and theological sense to select the first married men to be ordained from among these natural leaders who have already arisen.

But do we have to wait until they experience a 'vocation'

understood as a special call from God? We do not: for the call of the Church to fill such an office would already constitute a vocation. It is sometimes objected that such people 'could not dedicate the whole of their lives to God'. If the objection means that the only way to 'dedicate the whole of one's life to God' is by exclusive concentration on matters ecclesiastical, such as counting the collection or repairing the church roof, then it reveals a preposterously narrow view of the 'things of God'. They would be 'part-time' priests only in the sense that all priests are 'part-time': i.e. they are not, and cannot be, exercising the specifically priestly ministry all the time. Nor can an argument be based on the supposedly superior moral demands made on the priestly minister: whatever moral obligations are placed upon him, they cannot add to the moral obligations which are laid upon all Christians.

(4) A fourth consequence of applying the thinking of Vatican II to the ministry is that there should be some role for the congregation in the appointment of Parish priests and bishops. The old concept was that they should be simply parachuted down upon a grateful congregation. It was unintentionally satirized by Bishop Tourel of Montpellier who announced the news that an auxiliary bishop was to be named in his diocese in the following manner: 'Today I am able to pass on to you good tidings which fill me with joy. The Holy Father is giving me Fr Jean Orchampt as an auxiliary.' This conjures up a remarkable vision. It was as though, said Julian Walter, 'Fr Jean Orchampt had been flown by a stork direct from Rome and found one morning in the palace garden at Montpellier reclining under a gooseberry bush' (*The Month,* October 1971).

But the fact that bishops do not drop down from heaven has already been recognized in principle and in practice. That it is recognized in principle can be seen from the way in which 'consultations' preceded the appointment of, say, Cardinal Hume. No one knows exactly how the Apostolic Delegate, Mgr Bruno Heim, performed his delicate task or how he weighted the opinions he received, and he is not likely to tell us.[4] But the fact that he felt obliged to let the whole world

[4] Roman gossip, a notoriously unreliable source, suggests that this particular appointment was made against the wishes of the Congregation of Bishops and was due to the personal intervention of Archbishop Heim with Pope Paul. *Verb. sap.*

know that he had consulted means that some attempt was made to relate the appointment to the perceived needs of the Church in England.

What is here asserted in principle happens in practice in the nomination of parish priests: certain parishes have acquired a style of leadership—I'll name no names—such that it would be impossible to appoint an old-style autocratic priest to them; and he would not last long if he were appointed. Admittedly, these are only embryonic manifestations of the will to consult, but they are not negligible. From John Bossy's admirable book, *The English Catholic Community*. 1570–1850 (Darton, Longman and Todd, 1975), we discover that before the restoration of the hierarchy in 1850 there was a tendency among English Catholics to move towards a 'congregational' model in the appointment of parish priests, and that the priests themselves expected to elect their bishops. We would therefore perhaps be justified in thinking of the last 125 years of monarchical episcopacy as an interlude which is now drawing to a close.

(5) Finally, and in justice, a word must be said about where all this leaves the ordinary priest—if such a one exists. I assume someone who was ordained on the basis of one theology and who now finds another developing. I assume further that while he may find celibacy a sacrifice he does not find it an intolerable burden or a diminishment of his powers of self-giving. Such a man may well feel, to mix a few metaphors, that the castle walls are crumbling and that the rug is being pulled from under his feet. But provided he can get over initial defensiveness, he should be able to find in the new theology a firmer foundation and a stronger motivation for his priestly ministry. It is not diminished but enhanced by being set in the context of other ministries and related to the needs of the community. His task is not to run the show but, in the words of Fr David Woodward, 'to allow the Spirit to happen'. The priestly minister becomes the enabler of other ministries. I can envisage the celibate priests of the future making the contribution sometimes made by the religious orders today: with their greater mobility and independence, they will have the role of social and intellectual pioneers, out on the frontiers between Church and world.

These few modest suggestions are not put forward

dogmatically, still less demagogically. They seem to flow quite naturally from the post-conciliar emphasis on ministry rather than priesthood. It is sometimes said that 'progressive' theologians simply cause trouble by arousing desires which they know are unlikely to be fulfilled, and so prepare fresh disappointments; but that argument would imply that there is some special virtue in keeping one's head permanently buried in the sand. In any case, what is actually being done in certain parts of the Church anticipates already the future I have attempted to describe. Praxis precedes the reflection on it which we call theology. This is merely another way of saying that the experience of the Church and its needs can be read as one of the ways in which the Holy Spirit speaks to the Church today.

In an international Church there will always be arguments in favour of uniformity, and it will be constantly urged that a particular local Church cannot forge ahead because its example would affect neighbouring Churches and, through the media, the whole Church. This is perfectly true, but it also seems to condemn the Church to complete immobility and the consecration of the *status quo*. If the convoy is only allowed to move at the speed of the slowest ship, it will hardly get out of harbour. However, one must also concede that a completely anarchic or wild-cat development of new ministries would be more likely to issue in schism than renewal. It is for that reason that I spent so much time on the background to the ministry in order to show that there are already available, in post-conciliary theology, more open options than is sometimes thought. It would be tragic if the *kairos* or time of the Spirit was missed because we were prisoners of hide-bound formulations and imaginatively incapable of exploiting the wealth of tradition in terms of present needs.

4

Reflections on Ministry
Mary Tanner

Mary Tanner read theology at Birmingham University, and then lectured in Old Testament at the Universities of Hull and Bristol. She is at present lecturing part-time in the Old Testament at Westcott House, Cambridge.

Mrs Tanner is an Anglican, and has been particularly interested in women's ministry. She serves on the Faith and Order Commission of the WCC, and the Church of England Faith and Order Advisory Group. Mrs Tanner is married, with two small children.

It is good to be challenged from time to time to give an account of matters of the faith and order of the church and I am grateful for this challenge to reflect upon the factors which have led me to change, or rather not so much to change, as to develop my views about Christian ministry. The tradition in which I grew up seemed to hold out to me the view that ministry is something belonging to a group of men set aside for the purpose and ordered into a God-given hierarchical structure of bishops, priests and deacons, whose inherited tasks were somehow quite different from and unrelated to those of the congregations to whom they ministered. Again and again I found myself forced to ask questions of this tradition, sometimes stimulated by the changes already taking place in the church and sometimes as a result of a re-reading of the evidence of the New Testament and the Early Church. This has constantly been put to the test by the ministry as I experienced it as someone ministered to, and as someone exercising ministry in partnership with others.

At first the important questions about ministry appeared to me to centre mainly in the making relevant in the twentieth century of the structure of the ministry the Church of England had inherited at the Reformation. Indeed this has often appeared to be the form of the question posed by the Church itself in its many reports on ministry. The emphasis seems to have been on the structure of the ministry: how can we conform the office of a bishop to the order of deaconesses or other forms of accredited lay ministry?

But when we look at the New Testament and the evidence of the Early Church such questions about the structure of the ministry seem less and less central. Nowhere is the New Testament concerned primarily with the form of ministry; it never holds out a once for all blueprint which has to be taken over and applied in every situation. On the contrary, what the New Testament documents illustrate with their different reasons for being written, their difference of emphasis and their enormous variety, is the importance of certain principles of ministry; what the Canterbury Statement calls 'normative principles governing the purpose and function of all ministry'.[1] A. E. Harvey in his short but very useful book *Priest or President?* identifies at least four guiding principles of ministry in the New Testament.[2] There is the principle of being sent, the apostolic quality of ministry resting on Jesus' commission to his disciples; the principle of service, the diaconal aspect, not reserved for one special order of deacons but the responsibility of all; the principle of shepherding, of looking after the flock and the principle of exercising authority, though not in any narrow authoritarian way. Such principles are traceable back through the layers of New Testament tradition to Jesus himself and were earlier glimpsed by Israel in her attempts to understand her vocation. What is more they characterize the ministry of Jesus, for he is the One who is Sent, the Servant, the Shepherd and the One in Authority. In tracing these principles we see an oscillation between them as belonging on the one hand to the whole group of those who followed Jesus, to all the disciples, and on the other to a particularly chosen group of twelve, and in the case of exercising authority, belonging in some special way to Peter the leader of the Twelve. According to these principles ministry belongs to all, but some of its tasks more logically and appropriately are exercised by a few on behalf of all. In a flock it is not appropriate that all should shepherd, nor for all to exercise authority; and even when it comes to being sent out, not all are able to take up the challenge in the same way. This oscillation between what belongs to all and what to specially chosen leaders seems not to have been just an accident of

[1] The Canterbury Statement is the agreed statement on Ministry and Ordination by the Anglican–Roman Catholic International Commission. It was first published in 1973. *The Three Agreed Statements*, SPCK 1978.

[2] A. E. Harvey, *Priest or President?*, SPCK 1975. I am very grateful to A. E. Harvey's book for helping me to clarify my own thinking on the subject of ministry and I acknowledge a particular debt to him in the following discussion of the principles of ministry. Many of his conclusions I share and had already reached in preparing a series of lectures on ministry some four years ago.

history but is hinted at as necessary by Jesus himself in his own deliberate choice of the Twelve.

From the Acts onwards we have the picture of a group of people who were convinced by experience that they had been brought into a new relationship with God through Jesus, that they were the new people of God, the Body of Christ and that they had a mission to the world. We see this people growing in the power of the Spirit, being strengthened and moving outwards from Jerusalem. They inherited no hard and fast structure, but with certain principles to guide and a handful of already chosen leaders, they were able to respond to new and changing situations. There is some hint of the awareness of the need for continuity of leadership in the choice of Matthias to fill the place left by the death of Judas, and also in the example of Paul at Ephesus who appears to delegate responsibility to the twelve disciples there. In the absence of the Apostles the local churches were often placed under the rule of elders *(presbuteroi)*, or overseers *(episkopoi)* as they are at other times called. In the New Testament these words were used interchangeably. In Acts 20:28 Paul addresses the elders *(presbuteroi)* at Ephesus as shepherds *(episkopoi)*. In 1 Peter 5:2 the *presbuteroi* are told to tend the flock, exercising oversight. In Titus 1:5 Titus is told to appoint elders in every city in Crete and immediately a list is given of the qualifications of an *episkopos* and the appointment is said to be of *eposkopoi*. In addition to these there is mention of deacons. It is unlikely that the seven in Acts 5 are deacons in our sense of the word, for although they serve tables they are never called *diaconoi,* and the work that two of them subsequently undertake is much closer to the work of an Apostle than of a diaconal kind. Deacons are mentioned again in several epistles but without any clear indication of the nature of their work. Besides these leaders the early Christians detected amongst their number those who had different gifts and it was Paul's task to point out that no one gift was superior to another, whether the gift was for prophecy or teaching or healing or speaking with tongues; all were for the building up and strengthening of the whole church.

Just as no first-century evidence supports a blueprint of three orders of ministry, so the second-century evidence is short and scant and does not enable us to detect one universal pattern of ministry. Although Ignatius, Bishop of Antioch in 115, makes reference to a threefold order it is not until the third century that evidence for a threefold hierarchical structure emerges clearly as a universally accepted pattern. The evidence certainly does not support the preface to the Anglican Ordinal: 'It is evident to all men diligently reading Holy Scriptures and Ancient Authors, that from the Apostles time there have been three orders of ministry in Christ's Church: Bishops, Priests and Deacons.' In fact just where the evidence would need to be strongest to support a threefold ministry deriving from the Apostolic age—that is, at the very earliest period—it is here found to be the weakest. The picture of the early years is rather of a church still responding to the changes and demands of society with the emergence of a variety of supporting ministries in the minor orders. These included the sub-deacons to help with the distribution of alms, exorcists for visiting the mentally deranged, acolytes, readers, doorkeepers and two orders of women, the widows and the deaconesses.

This is obviously a very sketchy handling of evidence from the New Testament and the Early Church, but it is perhaps enough to show the sort of pointers which emerge when we attempt to let the material speak for itself rather than searching to find justification for our present practice of ministry in the pages of the New Testament. The important clues seem to me to be these; the ministry was that of Jesus which he delegated to all his followers for the building up of the community of the faithful and in turn for mission to the world. Such ministry was to embody certain 'normative principles', those which were already illustrated in Jesus' own earthly ministry. From the outset there was recognition of the need for leadership but no one pattern or structure appeared to be laid down or to dominate. There was recognition too of the need to let a number of diverse gifts flourish for the building up and strengthening of the whole Body. The picture is of a community responding to the age in which it lived, finding new expressions of ministry and new patterns as it sought to reach out in mission. Diversity and flexibility rather than uniform structure are what speak most forcibly. All this suggests that the question I at first thought important, of trying to make sense of a particular ministerial structure, is far from being the central issue and is one which can rightly be seen only in the context of a broader understanding of ministry. But such conclusions on their own would lead only to academic speculations. Reflection on the New Testament witness and the tradition of the church needs all the time to be measured and tested against our own experience. Our understanding must constantly be put to the test as we both experience ministry, as people ministered to, and no less as we exercise ministry in partnership with other Christians. Such experience in a number of parishes and specialist areas in different dioceses in England has confirmed me in the view that these New Testament clues are important and necessary for our contemporary situation. Although they have sometimes made me aware of the inadequacies of our present interpretation and exercise of ministry they have also convinced me of the tremendous resources and possibilities at the church's disposal if only we can make effective the theological insights which have been gained and are currently being discussed.

It can never be said too often that the ministry does not belong to the church, and least of all to a separated group of men; it is the ministry of Jesus himself carried out in and by the church, not for its own ends but for the world, that all might believe. Ministry belongs not to the few who are separated and ordained but to all the baptized.

It is only when we begin to unravel and work out in practice this vision of the ministry of the whole people of God that the place of separated ministry will be seen in its right perspective. Any attempt to describe how the ministry of every baptized person is worked out in practice is, of course, an impossibility. It will be as varied and different as the situations are different in which Christians find themselves living and working. The Church of England Report on the Diaconate made some attempt at describing it.[3] It suggested that some Christians will exercize their ministry in Church organizations such as Sunday schools or as members of the Parish Council, some will be involved in informal Christian organizations such as Christian Aid, and others will work for

---

[3] *Deacons in the Church.* The Report of a Working Party set up by the Advisory Council for the Church's Ministry, 1974. I learnt much from my fellow members of this working party as we struggled to assess the theological arguments relevant to this discussion and to consider the practical working of the diaconate as it is exercised in our church at the present day.

secular voluntary bodies such as the Samaritans or Shelter. But 'most Christians perform most of their work of ministry in the "given" structures of modern secular society in which they are inextricably immersed, rather than in Church structures or indeed in voluntary structures of any kind. Parents in their families, shop-keepers in their stores, bankers in their banks, policemen in their districts, teachers in their schools, actors in their theatres or T.V. studios, cooks in their cafés—these should be the people of God serving him in the world. And if they cannot achieve something here, what will it avail if they occasionally help with Church work?

'It is very important to emphasize that such a ministry in and to secular structures is not just a matter of a high standard of personal living. Christian people are called not only to love and respect those people with whom they have personal contact, but also to strive for justice for many thousands and, indeed, millions of human beings whom they can never know personally at all. This means not only a "ministry to people" with whom we have a personal contact but also a "ministry to structures", to the complicated and sometimes threatening economic, social and political structures which dominate modern society.'

The church needs constantly to remind people of the centrality of the belief in the ministry of the laity and to search out new methods of education and create opportunities for discussion. We must demonstrate both the everyday ways as well as the more spectacular in which ministry can be exercised. Sometimes it will be necessary to encourage Christians to make new commitments to take up new ventures; sometimes it will mean helping people to identify ways in which they are already, perhaps unconsciously, exercising ministry, so that they may become more effective and purposeful. One thing is clear, for all our lip service to the idea, we have not begun adequately to unpack the implications contained in the phrase the ministry of the laity.'

It is the laity who are the spearhead of ministry, for they can reach out day by day to the many areas where ordained or even professional lay ministry may never reach. But the necessity for set-apart leaders is clearly pointed to in the New Testament and lies in the very humanness of the church as an organization. We see in the New Testament leaders, whether *presbuteroi* or *episkopoi,* coming to hold authority, some-times delegated by an Apostle. This seems to point to an early emerging pattern of a group of leaders, in some way related to and dependent upon a smaller group which perhaps can be seen as pointing to our later relationship between bishop and priest. Such a separated group is important for the organiza-tion of the community, but more than this they are a focus of the unity and continuity of the church. It is not easy to define with any finality the particular ministry of the ordained and certainly no one word can be found to sum it up. It needs a whole cluster of words to get anywhere near an adequate picture. *The set-apart ministry must embody, focus, represent, demonstrate, uphold, take a lead in at least those principles of ministry we detect as belonging to the ministry in the New Testament; in particular of being sent, of serving, of shepherd-ing and of exercising authority.*

The actual tasks in which these principles comes to life will be, like the task of the laity, too numerous and diverse to outline and they must obviously vary from age to age. Being sent must involve going out to proclaim the Good News, continuing until the world confesses that Jesus is Lord. Serv-ing must involve caring for those within the fellowship of the church and outside, caring especially for the downtrodden and suffering, following the pattern of Jesus' own ministry. Shepherding must involve leading the church so that it is built up into a living fellowship, and because of the kind of com-munity it is it will be built up in and through its worship and particularly in the celebration of the Eucharist. Exercising authority points in the direction of a separated ministry entrusted with the power to regulate the organizational life of the church, and more important to exercise the power dele-gated by Christ, through his Apostles, to forgive and in some cases bind sins; a priestly principle will be focused in the leading of the offering of lives in service, and in the offering of sacrifices of praise and thanksgiving, as well as in calling to mind the once for all sacrifice of Christ by presiding at the Eucharist. This description of what the separated ministry might undertake is only the very beginnings of drawing out functions from the principles. It only begins to hint at the variety of tasks which might belong to the minister. There is a whole bundle of interrelated tasks which go to make up the ministerial office and to give a job description would be an impossibility.

Important as it is to hold together ordained and lay ministry it is not easy to spell out exactly what that relationship should be. Again there is no one word which captures the relationship completely; it needs many words and ideas before it begins to be clear. The two are partners in ministry, not one superior to the other, equal partners; there is a sense in which they are leaders and led; stimulators and stimulated; encouragers and encouraged, but perhaps the most useful pair of words to hold on to is 'enablers and enabled'. The ordained must concentrate on leading, enabling, encouraging, and stimulating the laity to be the spearhead of ministry, recognizing that it can never be left to their own small and currently diminishing numbers. This may mean less of their time being spent on keeping the plant going and more delegation of this part of their work. I am sometimes horrified by the amount of time the clergy spend on the fabric of the parish churches when there are more competent and qualified lay Christians who should be encouraged to take over this aspect of their work. Much more the ordained ministry must look for appropriate ways to stimulate and enable. They must try to hold before the laity the challenges of new ideas and new possibilities for practical discipleship and create opportunities for people to discuss and argue them. While the opportunity and stimulus for discussion on ministry can be provided by the minister, new ways will be found only in dialogue with those involved in the world outside the church. Leadership in the context of the Gospel is not achieved by telling others what to do as much as in setting them free to come to their own decisions. The ordained must look for ways for people to become committed to new truths and to act upon them. They should investigate how structures or cells for support and fellowship can be established to help people put ideas into practice.

This, then, is only the beginning of a picture of the ways in which the set-apart ministry can lead lay ministry into being a more effective spearhead of ministry in the world, and in the process of developing this aspect of their ministry new patterns will emerge. Such stimulation will result in a variety of new groupings of lay and ordained, sometimes within the

parochial structure, sometimes across it. We are all so different, that few of us belong happily to the same type or even
size of group. Some need discipline imposed by a group,
others need less and would feel threatened by the need for
over-commitment to one group in a life of many commitments. We cannot begin to picture all the types of groups or
the different actions which might result from the stimulation
and challenge of new ideas, but flexibility and adaptability
must always be the mark and test of such initiatives. Only in
such ways will the set-apart ministry be true shepherds, helping, enabling and supporting the laity to understand and
perform their mission in the world.

While they explore ways of stimulating the laity to be an
effective spearhead of ministry, they must always seek to
build up the fellowship of the Body of Christ by word and
sacrament. It is in the Eucharist, presided over by the
ordained and assisted by the lay, that they are most truly the
Body of Christ united together and united with the church
universal. It is from here that they are driven out to the
contemporary world in the power of the Spirit with their task
of mission confirmed, and to this they return.

There is, of course, another aspect of this relationship
between the ordained and lay. The relationship must never be
one way. The laity need to understand the support of action,
prayer and indeed of obedience which they owe to their
leaders. The life of the unsupported leader, of whom so much,
often too much, is expected, can be very lonely. Two interesting articles in the *Church Times* some three years ago—one by
a bishop the other by a parish priest—made this point very
emphatically and began to spell out the ways in which congregations can be expected to be more effective supporters of
their leaders. So with a rightly renewed assertion of the ministry of the laity must come an exploration of this two-way
relationship, not just in abstract terms, but in ways in which
such a relationship can be put into practice.[4]

The New Testament points us then in the direction of
understanding ministry as Christ's, which he delegates to all

[4] It is interesting to note that the Methodist Conference has recently (1977)
adopted a report on 'The Pastoral Care of the Ministry', showing how much need
there is for help, not least in family matters, and how much the laity can help and
support if they are willing to do so.

Christians, and it is within this context that it points to the necessity for a separated ministry. We have seen that there are other New Testament clues for ministry today. Two important characteristics are clearly the flexibility and diversity of ministry. Paul insists that there are diverse gifts of ministry: teaching, prophecy, healing, utterance and so on; but the New Testament also points to a growing diversity of ministry associated with particular needs. Deaconesses, for example, prepare women candidates for baptism; and other tasks are associated with widows, doorkeepers, acolytes, readers and sub-deacons.

There are two lessons here. The church needs much more to expect such gifts, even the spontaneous, and to encourage them; has prophecy ceased, and why are so many of us so suspicious of the signs of a charismatic renewal or of a ministry of healing or exorcism? We must also expect and encourage new and experimental forms of lay ministry. The Church of England has a group of Accredited Lay Workers, its Deaconesses, Church Army Captains and Sisters, Licensed Lay Workers and Church Social Workers and Readers. Many of these groups emerged to meet the uncared for needs of society at the end of the last century and the beginning of this. Some of these needs are now the concern of the Welfare State and so the reason for a particular form of Accredited Lay Ministry may well have disappeared. But as society changes, new areas of need are created and one of the concerns of professional lay ministry must be to be the ministry of the gaps, concentrating on identifying and ministering in areas not covered by the statutory agencies. It must seek out new areas and provide new patterns of care and be prepared to move on if and when the State takes over. Help for battered wives, for mothers tempted to batter their children, and care for the homeless and the unemployed and their families spring to mind as areas of need in contemporary society. Accredited Lay Ministry should be adaptable and flexible enough to fill the gaps. Instead of putting all professional lay ministry under one umbrella in a newly identified or reconstructed diaconate, a third Order of separated ministry, as has sometimes been advocated in recent years, we should concentrate on producing a proliferation of ministries, of groups with specialist expertise and training. Perhaps a group specializing in Christian Education, and one with a renewed interest in church social work. One of the important values of professional lay ministry should be that it is more adaptable, more flexible than ordained ministry. It can afford to take greater risks, as it is not called upon in the same way to embody and exercise authority which properly belongs to the ordained. It should never seek to justify itself or seek validation by aping the role of the ordained.

There is obviously one great difficulty which perhaps restricts Accredited Lay Ministry in the Church of England developing freely at the present time. While the ordained ministry is exclusively male, Accredited Lay Ministry is largely female. From a recent survey of women engaged in it, it is clear that many of them would seek ordination if that were possible. Until this is resolved, and the final legal barriers removed and women are able to share fully in ordained ministry, it seems unlikely that the church will be in a position to see clearly ways in which to develop professional lay ministry and what the relationship between it and ordained ministry might be. Only then will there be a situation in which a complementary male/female ordained ministry will find a counterpart and support in an equally complementary male/female accredited lay ministry.

So my reading of the New Testament and church history with the help of so much excellent modern scholarship, together with my experience of ministry, have moved me far from the narrow pyramid view of ministry, with its emphasis on the maleness of ministry with which I began, to a conviction that what is important is a circular view of ministry in which every Christian is called to play a part. Diversity must characterize the ministry: there will be men and women; ordained and lay; accredited and non-accredited; professional and non-professional; part-time and full-time; some will minister in close identification and association with church structures, others will be less closely related; some will make life commitments, others not; some ministries will be prepared for, others will be spontaneous. Flexibility must be the other important feature as the church seeks to relate the ministry of Christ to people wherever they are. Only with a ministry that is diverse and flexible can the church really hope to be effective in mission and to reach out to the maximum in mission.

Such a view of ministry inevitably raises particular questions about the role of the laity in the liturgical life of the community. It is raised, not only in relation to the part which Accredited Lay Ministry should play, but to the part of all Christians. The belief in the ministry of the laity ought to be in some ways reflected in the life of the worshipping community, particularly in the central act of the Eucharist. Recent years have seen the increase of liturgical function for the laity. Many churches have already made efforts to involve the congregations, with members reading lessons, offering the prayer for the church and bringing the bread and wine to the altar. Although the ordained must be the one who holds together the ministry of word and sacrament in each place, there might be provided more occasions for the laity to preach and expound their own views on the relation of the Gospel to daily living. There is being heard with increasing regularity a request for lay celebration. This is a question the church will have to face in the near future, particularly if there is to be a renewed emphasis on the ministry of the laity. It is a difficult issue and one for which the New Testament does not give us an easy answer. At what particular time the celebration of the Eucharist came to be reserved to the ordained is not clear and our early sources are again fragmentary. Ignatius in the second century tells the Christians at Smyrna 'that they ought not, apart from the Bishop, either to baptize or hold a love feast', but from the third century onwards the tradition is firm that it is the right and duty of the ordained. In any human organization it is customary for the chairperson to preside at a meeting and to hold ultimate responsibility for the traditions of that company. Similarly it seems we should argue that as the Eucharist is the central activity of the church's life, the point at which the community is knit together as one body in Christ, the one who presides must be the person who feels himself called and whose call is recognized by the church in ordination as the one responsible for shepherding and bearing authority. To take this central act away from the ordained minister would be to undermine his peculiar role in the life of the church at the very point at which it needs to be focused. Such a view has recently been stated in the Canterbury Statement on the Eucharist, the Agreed Anglican/Roman Catholic Statement. 'The central act of worship, the Eucharist, is the memorial of that reconciliation and nourishes the church's life for the fulfilment of its mission. Hence it is right that he who has oversight in the church and is the focus of its unity should preside at the celebration of the Eucharist.'[5] I believe that the ordained minister should preside at the Eucharist in order to safeguard the handing on of the central mystery of the Body but, even then, he should be seen to be supported and helped by the laity in the fullest possible way. At the same time I am beginning to question whether the order of the church would be seriously threatened if on occasions this central act is delegated directly by an ordained minister to a responsible and thoroughly prepared member of the laity. There are a few occasions when a closely-knit fellowship of lay-Christians, involved in a common enterprise of education or pastoral care, takes on a life of its own and it seems unnatural to 'import' an ordained minister to celebrate the Eucharist. This is one of the questions the church will need to look at in the future.

With such growing convictions about ministry comes also a confirmation of the value of the parochial structure and the possibilities which exist there to live out such an understanding of ministry. It seems self-evident to say that everyone in England lives in a parish, but often we do not realize what a potential we have inherited in this. The parochial structure does offer the possibility of reaching out to people where they live and of supporting them in their everyday needs. However encumbered we may feel by difficult and sometimes unwieldy buildings, these are resources which can be used for the local community. It is in the parish, with its delineated area and its buildings, that we have an opportunity to make shared ministry a reality. The parochial minister has an important role to play, not because he is an omnicompetent parish priest capable of carrying out all the many and diverse tasks of the inherited 'bundle', but because he is the enabler of ministry in that place. For this end he must be a man of prayer and a man of scholarship who can think theologically about the church and the world, but he may well not be the best administrator, leader of clubs, visitor or even teacher or preacher. He must

---

[5] *An Agreed Statement on Eucharistic Doctrine*, SPCK 1972. This is again the work of the Anglican–Roman Catholic International Commission which was completed at Windsor in 1971.

be capable of a wide vision of what ministry in that particular area might mean and be capable of conveying and encouraging that vision; someone open to people, who can recognise their many talents and see that they are used, whether in the direct service of the church or of the wider community. He must identify who has the gift of teaching, of musicianship, of caring, of listening, of greeting others, or even of making tea, and see that all gifts are encouraged for the building up of the Body. In such a way the parochial minister should not be so concerned with developing his own ministry as creating a team ministry in that place. Together, lay and ordained can be involved in teaching and preaching, in caring for and visiting the sick and old, in supporting the bereaved, in welcoming people into the fellowship, and in being given to hospitality. Some congregations are already exploring such shared ministry, others not, and it would be of great value if we could learn more often from one another and share new ideas and ways of working. It may well be that some parishes need to look outside themselves for help in particular areas. It is obvious that some are more blessed in lay leadership than others. They may need the help of an Accredited Lay Minister with specialist knowledge. Here the diosecan structure is important, for it can be a resource centre for ministry with teams of experts or at least people with knowledge of where such expertise exists. It may be because of being related to an area church which can feed them and in turn be fed by them.

I have come to hope and expect that my parish priest will be someone who will help and encourage me to play a part in the church's ministry, to show me the needs of the local church and the ways in which I can support and help him with other Christians in meeting those needs, in the first place to build up the fellowship of the church though constantly reminded that that is not an end in itself. This conviction of the importance of parochial ministry in stimulating the ministry of the whole church, is not an abstract theory, but one which has again and again been proved to work in experience.

Such insistence on the value of parochial ministry does not mean, of course, that the church should not develop its pattern of specialist or sector posts, for it is here also that the diversity of ministry can be attested. Rightly underlying the growth in the number of specialist ministries is a recognition that the church has a duty to minister to people wherever they are and not only where they live; a mission and ministry to social structures, whether local government, political groups, educational structures, industrial organizations, entertainment or communications. Although much of this work can be done only by the ministry of every Christian, the advocates of specialist posts believe the church is only seen to be committed when its clergy are committed. A recent Church of England report on specialist ministries urged that 'new areas of ministry should be opened up constantly, meeting people in their weakness, drug addicts, immigrants and the mentally ill, in their strength as with police, teachers or scientists and also in *ad-hoc* situations in theatres or stores'. There does seem to be currently a real attempt in a growing number of these posts to search out new areas of need and to adapt ministry to serve them. There is also some sign that in some experiments a pattern is emerging of the specialist minister being actively supported by a lay team. There is the example of a curate who has a specialized evangelistic mission, travelling around the country leading missions and being supported in this work by a group of twenty-five lay people who help by prayer and finance, and who sometimes join the evangelistic team with him. 'The evangelist is nothing without the team, nor the team without the evangelist' was a comment written about this. Another example of such experiment is of a vicar who, with the approval of his bishop, now devotes all his time to exorcism, prayer and faith healing and for whom support has come from a group of lay people who have set up a trust to provide a house and income for this ministry to continue. The emergence of such specialist ministries with the supportive backing, both by prayer and finance of lay people, seems to me another significant step in the right direction. It shows ordained and lay working closely together and may well hold a clue for the future. It is a pity when those in traditional parochial roles feel threatened by a growing number of specialist posts of whatever kind. Perhaps much more thought should be given to developing the idea that the parochial situation is itself a specialist situation, embracing the different patterns of urban and rural parishes: the country parson needs his own particular field of expertise which must be quite different from that of the priest on a new housing estate or an inner-city area. What is more, the work of a parish priest can itself be broken down into many parts, counselling, comforting the bereaved, training for confirmation, preparing for marriage, etc. It might perhaps help if one parish priest in a diocese were an expert in one field and made his knowledge available widely. All this points in the same direction; to a ministry which is diverse, flexible, interrelated, supportive, and in which ordained and lay work closely together.

My thoughts so far have been very much from an Anglican perspective though much is applicable to other churches. There is however one final growing conviction that I have gained directly as a result of experience; that is of the growing ecumenical possibilities of ministry. If experience has suggested this, the New Testament with Jesus' prayer that we should be one, confirms it as an imperative to seek after. Common sense too suggests the ambiguity in the church offering to the world a word of reconciliation and healing when its approach is broken and divided. The situation in England at present holds out enormous possibilities for ecumenical ministry as the churches in their official discussions move closer together. Already there are Areas of Ecumenical Experiment where ministers and congregations are working together in the closest possible ways. There are dioceses in which new experiments in lay ministry are being worked out ecumenically. In the West Country, for example, there has been in existence for some time an Ecumenical Order of Teachers, where lay people of all denominations train together in a rigorous way to undertake a responsibility in the locality for the church's teaching ministry. In this new and growing order, the brain-child of a lay woman, lay and ordained work together in the closest ecumenical way and those who experience such a close working together in ministry can feel the building up of the unity for which we seek. At parochial and diocesan levels and in some of our theological colleges, the ecumenical possibilities of ministry are being experienced and developed further. But the situation is very uneven over the country and much more publicity is needed to encourage those areas where ecumenical ministry has not taken root. It is not enough for congregations to take part in the week of prayer for Christian Unity or for the clergy of an area to meet together for prayer. There must be a full and sustained involvement of ordained and lay in all areas of ministry and a further extension of ecumenical parishes. Now is the time for exchanging information about our experiences and experiments with forms of lay ministry and sector ministries, and perhaps even more important, a time for the Church of England to learn from the many years' experience that some of the Free Churches have had of women in ordained ministry. The next years must be a time for creative thinking and experimenting in new ecumenical patterns so that, as the churches come closer together theologically, they may express this in the practice of their ministry.

Such convictions about and hopes for ministry are not intended as harsh criticism of the church. Indeed there are many signs that the church, in spite of its often cumbersome organization that would tie it to a past age, is trying to make sense of ministry and fruitfully experimenting. Reflection and experiment must continue so that ministry can become as diverse and flexible as possible. In particular the church must face contemporary challenges: the growing demand for the ordination of women to the priesthood; a renewal of forms of lay ministry; the growing possibilities for ecumenical ministry and the demand for lay celebration. We must not be timid but, taking our example from the church of the Acts of the Apostles, move forward under the power and guidance of the Spirit, being confirmed in the belief that the ministry we share and seek to understand more fully is the ministry of Him who came not to be ministered to but to minister and to give His life a ransom for many.

TEOO—4 **

5

More Ministry or More Priests?

Tony Barnard

Born in Somerset in 1936, Tony Barnard was educated at Christ's Hospital, and after National Service took degrees in Natural Science and Theology at St John's College, Cambridge. After two years at Wells Theological College, he was ordained to a title in Cheshunt, Hertfordshire, in 1963. Two years later he returned to Wells as Tutor, lecturing in Old Testament, subsequently becoming Vice-Principal and being also involved in In-service training for clergy and lay education. With the merger of Wells and Salisbury Colleges, he became Vice-Principal of the new College in 1972, and in 1974 Director of the Non-Residential training programme for Auxiliary Ministry in the Southern Dioceses, and later worked to develop the Bishop's Certificate in Christian Education. In 1977 he was appointed Canon Chancellor of Lichfield Cathedral, with responsibility for developing ministry and training in the Diocese.

Mr Barnard is married, with three children.

Apart from the periods during and immediately after the two world wars, there has not been a time, in the recent history of the Anglican church, when so few men have been ordained to the priesthood. In the early 1960s there was a dramatic fall in the number offering themselves for ordained ministry; a fall which has more or less continued ever since, and can be paralleled in other branches of the church. In numerical terms, whereas 988 men attended selection conferences in 1963 of which 737 were recommended for training, parallel figures in 1965 were 655 and 472, and whereas 636 were ordained Deacon in 1963, there were only 373 ten years later. It is small wonder then, that with earlier retirement, and the average age of clergy well into the fifties, there is an overall decline in the number of priests in the Church of England. In his enthronement sermon, the present Archbishop of Canterbury pointed to this fact and expressed the hope that it could be remedied, a hope that has been echoed by many others. Important questions, however, remain—'What sort of ministry are we looking for, and how are we hoping to recruit for it?' If the answer to these questions was once obvious, it is so no longer, and the wealth of published material from writers and theologians, as from national and diocesan working parties is evidence of this.[1]

[1] A survey of much recent Anglican material will be found in Hugh Melinsky, *Patterns of Ministry* (GS 202, Church Information Office).
Other Reports include:
1964   *Partners in Ministry*
1968   *A Supporting Ministry* (CIO)
       Women in Ministry (CIO)
1969   *Ordained Ministry Today* (CIO)
1971   *Bishops and Dioceses* (CIO)
1972   *Local Ministry in Urban and Industrialised Areas* (Mowbrays)
       Priests in Secular Employment. Not Published.

Parochial priesthood was once the norm. A man felt called to exercise a ministry in a limited geographical area, to a community of people clustered round the parish church. The rural village community was the ideal, and featured in many an ordinand's vision of the future. Priesthood was, too, seen by many as the ultimate expression of discipleship. One has interviewed so many people who have always wanted to be ordained and who feel that the ways open to them of expressing their commitment are inadequate. The call to priesthood came in many different ways. Some were undoubtedly influenced by the example of priests they knew. Men of great piety, zeal, love and vision, largely unconsciously encouraged others to join their ranks. Time and again, there have been notable men in the church who were indirectly responsible for large numbers of vocations, and still today, it is noticeable how a particular parish, and surely a particular incumbent, may have a long list of ordinands. Others, however, were attracted to the priesthood by seeing it as the obvious channel for their desire to love and help others through a pastoral ministry, or perhaps to lead worship and to preach. In contrast, yet a third group were undoubtedly attracted towards ordination through a sense of discontent with the Established Church and the inadequacy of church life as they experienced it, and so with a vocation to reform and renew. So the paths by which the Holy Spirit led men to offer themselves for ordination might be various, the ideal of priesthood, to which they were attracted was clear, and parochial priesthood was the norm by which they identified their sense of vocation. Today, however, this is far too limited a view of ministry and of the routes to it. Although the overall picture is far from clear there are three main areas in which change is being effected.

There is a change, first, in our understanding of the *nature of ministry*. Priesthood has, in the past, been thought of, not exclusively, but largely, in representational terms. The priest

1973   *Ordination of Women to the Priesthood* (GS 104A)
       The Place of Auxiliary Ministry, Ordained and Lay (CIO)
1974   *Local Ministry* (ACCM Occasional Paper No. 1)
1975   *A Survey of Accredited Lay Ministry* (ACCM Occasional Paper No. 2)
       The Ministry of the People of God (ACCM Occasional Paper No. 3)
1976   *The Deployment of the Clergy* (GS 205, 258, 308)
1977   *An Honorary Ministry* (ACCM Occasional Paper No. 8)
       The Ministry of Deacons and Deaconesses (GS 344).

was God's representative to the people, and represented them before God. Today, priesthood is more and more being considered in functional terms, those functions being defined by the needs of the community, which is served. Secondly, and in the light of this change, *the work of ministry* is being thought of less exclusively in terms of the leading of worship and of pastoral care by the individual and greater emphasis given to the sharing of the very divers functions needed to equip the church for its work. And thirdly, this shift in emphasis is being reflected in a reassessment of the nature of *vocation*. In the past, the emphasis has been on the community's recognition of the individual's call, through the episcopal laying on of hands, today there is growing recognition that the community could and should be more active in delegating ministry to its members. It may be worth looking at these changes in a little more detail.

The nature of ministry has, in the recent past—for fashions have surely changed in the church's long history—been determined by attention to only one of the many models available in the New Testament. By emphasizing the ministry of the word and of the sacraments, and identifying these largely with preaching and the celebration of the Eucharist, the church has stressed the representational aspect of ministry. The continuity between Jesus, the early apostles and the threefold order of bishop, priest and deacon was seen as of primary importance, and emphasized at the expense of the notions of ministry reflected in the writings of Paul and others in the early church, and indeed within the Old Testament community. More and more today, it is being realized that it is the whole church, which is the 'Body of Christ' and continues his ministry and that there is an important distinction between the ministry of that body to the world, and the ministry to that body which equips it for its work. Talk about the nature of ministry today, therefore, is talk not about the priesthood and the sparing delegation of certain aspects to trusted lay people, but about a rediscovery of the mission of the church, and the ministry which this requires.

The mission of the church occurs directly and indirectly. It occurs directly when Christians are able to speak about their faith, and to identify the work of God in their local situation. It occurs indirectly, when they can co-operate with the structures and movements within society which ameliorate the life of man, and when the way of life of the individual and of the community challenge and convict the world of the power and the presence of God. Thus ministry may be seen as a matter of word and deed for the individual and for the community, as this mission of the church is undertaken and the purpose of God achieved. It is the responsibility of the whole church and requires that individuals are ready to proclaim and to apologize for the faith, to prophesy and to interpret, and to back their word by a way of life which is self-authenticating. If this ministry *of* the church is to be effective, then it requires a ministry *to* the church, which will 'equip God's people for work in his service' (Eph. 4:12). Inevitably, there is a proper sense in which this ministry to the church is the responsibility of all Christians, as we minister to one another, but in a fuller and important sense this is the ministry of those trained and recognized. If in this way, we start from a consideration of the purpose of the church, which is its mission, then ministry is seen first as a total responsibility, and secondly as largely, though not exclusively, functional rather than representational.

It follows from this consideration of the nature of ministry that the *works of ministry* will be defined by the need to equip God's people. The past emphasis on liturgy and pastoral care must be supplemented today by the recognition of the need for teachers, prophets, and evangelists within the ministry, in order that the confidence and competence of lay people may be built up. Yet we may go further than this and recognize that by whatever means this is being achieved within the community, ministry is being exercised. In this way a ministry of group leadership or indeed of prayer, music and drama may be seen as functional aspects of the whole ministry of the church, building up the life of the individual and of the community. This broadening of the notion of the ministry to the church, which is not new but the redressing of an imbalance, may be matched by a broadening of our view of those who will undertake the work. Pastoral care has for some time been seen to be no longer the unique preserve of the priest in a community, and it is being increasingly realized that many other functions of ministry may be undertaken by people other than those ordained in the church. This, in turn, has implications for our understanding of *vocation*. The church has largely relied, in the past, on the personal call. If, however, what has been said so far has any force, then in the future the call may need to come as much from the community. There is a growing feeling that it is a proper notion for a Christian community to discern its needs and to discern its resources, calling out those with particular gifts and equipping them to exercise ministry.

In these three areas, then, we may discern a dramatic change in the understanding of the ministry of the church. It is a change which will be resisted by many, and certainly not all would agree with this summary of the present situation. It is a view of ministry which contrasts radically with the view with which I and my contemporaries embarked on ministry fifteen to twenty years ago. And that fact prompts another question. Why do some people see the need for change, while others do not? Why would some people see things much as they have been described above and others emphatically deny that this is what is happening? The answer to this question seems to lie in the realm of personal experience. There is no centrally agreed Anglican view of ministry today, and it is probably true to say that there is not even a Diocesan view. The church is characterized at the moment by a very localized view of ministry, and one's reaction to what is happening will be coloured very much by one's personal experience of the church and its work. Since it is the intention that the contributions to this symposium should be, in part, autobiographical, it may be worth considering some of the experiences which have led this writer to the conclusions outlined above.

A Developing View of Ministry

In the mid-50s, young men were sent out of Anglican theological colleges with a pretty clear idea of their job. A curacy in one area, under a good training-vicar, would be followed by one in a contrasting area, before a first living was offered. The work was varied but largely liturgical and pastoral. Visiting was important, and it was believed that 'a house-going parson made a church-going people'. Ten years later, things were beginning to be very different. It was the time of *Soundings, Objections to Christian Belief,* of *Honest to God,* the *New English Bible* and 'Series I.' The curates going into our parishes were less inclined to accept the traditional pattern of life and ministry, and found themselves ministering to congregations who were beginning to ask questions, and living amongst people who more openly rejected the church and its teachings. Quite apart from a desire to question what was going on, it was easy to feel that one's view of the ministry was seriously inadequate. I served my own title in an urban residential area north of London. My section of a large parish of nearly 20,000 centred on a tin-hut mission church surrounded by a population growing towards 9,000, living on private and council estates. An enthusiastic, small congregation contained elements which together reflected the history of the area. There were those who attended evensong regularly and communion once a month, whose allegiance to this building dated back to its early days, when it was run by the laity, and the curate celebrated communion occasionally. There were those who were weekly communicants, who had moved on to the new estates as they were built some thirty or more years later. With other minor variations, they made up a congregation which was all too seldom present together. My predecessor had the reputation of having visited every house in the area, and my notion of priesthood made me ambitious to follow his example. How quickly the vision went. It was impossible if one was to do more than put a foot in the door, and very quickly a list of priorities had to be developed. Baptism visits, since it was the early days of the development of a more rigorous policy about this, the newcomers, the sick, elderly and the congregation drew my attention, and the possibility of lay visiting teams to make up the deficiency immediately presented itself. Yet if they were to do this, they needed training. How often it was said that they had had no real teaching since confirmation classes twenty or thirty years ago, and so felt a lack of confidence faced by the need to visit on the church's behalf. At the same time, the early stewardship campaigns emphasizing the need for financial support of the church and its work, were giving way to campaigns involving time and talents, and further suggesting ways of developing lay ministry. Thus in these early days of ministry, a growing feeling of the inadequacy of the view held at ordination was beginning to find some compensation in a view of ministry that included the laity. Inevitably the function of the ordained minister began to change in understanding, as the demand grew for teaching, training and discerning the gifts of others within the body. When, after two years, I returned to my Theological College to teach Old Testament, it was with a different view of ministry from that with which I was equipped by that same college. The practice of ministry had begun to sharpen, refine and correct my understanding of my vocation. Life in a theological community was to develop this understanding further.

Anglican theological colleges developed mainly in the nineteenth century, basing their academic style on the university and their lifestyle, more on the monastery. Wells Theological College in the 1960s was under a Principal of great sensitivity and vision, and changed radically during its final decade (it merged with the College in Salisbury during 1971–2). The majority of students being young and single, colleges in the 50s, and in many cases for some time after this, were paternalistic and rigidly disciplined. The staff were a group apart and the Principal was the father-figure of the establishment. Worship could take place five or six times a day, and an apology to the Principal was expected for absence. This authority pattern matched that of the parish, with the vicar, his curates and the people, and, indeed, of the church at large. At Wells, however, the staff's misgivings about this pattern were given real form by a visit to Pontigny, where the relaxed style of this seminary of the 'Mission de France' encouraged a restructuring of college life after a first visit, and of the academic study after a subsequent one. The resulting pattern allowed the staff to become far more of a team, directed and enabled by the Principal, and did much to lessen the barrier between staff and student. The use of Christian names, for example, though in some ways a small thing, was indicative of a much greater willingness to treat the previous experience of students as important, to be concerned with developing our inter-relationships within the community, and to attend to the development of the individual spiritually and pastorally, as well as academically. It also resulted in the student being presented with a more open style of leadership and ministry. At the same time, a change from lectures and tutorials to a seminar system of study, encouraged real discussion, participation and the exchange of ideas, and an openness between individuals and towards a given subject. Although they can be recorded only in outline, these changes were important, in so far as they engendered attitudes within the training of ordinands, which were markedly different from the past and, I believe, peculiarly appropriate to the changing pattern of church life. It is surely not too much to claim that by becoming more conscious of the individuality of the student, and by a willingness to explore together ministry, theology and worship we were developing the capacity to send out young priests, who would explore the Christian faith and its implications with their people, rather than dictate patterns of belief and behaviour.

Subsequent developments in theological education have confirmed this early shift in emphasis. In keeping with educational theory, training by discovery has begun to mark the academic style of many more colleges, with a shift away from lectures and towards seminars, and an attempt to reflect on experience and relate study to ministry. At Salisbury the development of the Elephant and Castle scheme, and an emphasis on group training and communication, ensured that the merger with Wells would be a genuine match. The 'Elephant Scheme' is of particular interest. In the old days, pastoral training was given largely through the odd hour of parish visiting and through hospital work. At Salisbury, another imaginative Principal, Harold Wilson, conceived the idea of sending all students for a six-week period in the inner city in the hope that the questions raised by this experience would vitalize their studies at college. Students spent time investigating the local community, its needs and the church's response, and latterly, working with a growing number of agencies in the London area. Many thereby discovered a new dimension in the church's life, and the experience of radically different approaches to church activity and ministry was a formative one. Once again, these movements within the college, which have been very briefly sketched, inevitably influenced my own views of ministry reinforcing the sense of a need for diversification, for co-operation within the ministry and of the value of a model for ministry which encouraged exploration and openness. The influence of college life has not stopped there, however, since increasingly, colleges have been involved in more divers forms of training for ministry.

More Ministry or More Priests?

Prompted by Frank West, then Bishop of Taunton, a number of priests in the Diocese of Bath and Wells began in the mid-60s offering series of evening lectures at local technical colleges. It was something of a surprise to discover that fifty or sixty people would turn out week after week to listen to lectures on Biblical Criticism, for example, and to show a real interest in and, indeed, a thirst for knowledge. This desire, to be better informed, may be seen as the natural corollary to the growing pressure on them to be involved in the wider work of the church. A more systematic response to this need came in the development of an educational programme for the Ecumenical Order of Teachers in the same diocese. Founded by Miss Dorothy Daldy, herself in education work all her life, the movement sought to equip those who felt that with the laity demanding instruction in the faith and its implications, the resources amongst lay people could be better utilized by the church. For those with theological training and/or educational ability, an Order of Teachers seemed the obvious answer. A three-year course of academic study and practical experience was devised, in the hope that a proportion of those attending might share in the teaching ministry of the church. Over the last decade, a number of courses have developed through Christian institutes, extramural departments and similar institutions, which have similarly sought to equip lay people for a wider ministry. The excitement amongst them, which one has seen and shared, as a new vision of discipleship develops, has been a major personal influence in promoting concern for a change in our view of the church's ministry. Here are people who have been for too long enslaved and are beginning to realize their potential. Yet here it is probably important to add certain qualifications.

It is surely undeniable that the Anglican Church has depended for too long on ministry solely, or largely, through its ordained priesthood. Most of us will find some humour but also some truth in the suggestion that we must be prepared to preach, teach, visit and care, to administer and keep the accounts, and if necessary to mow the grass in the churchyard and paint the down-pipes! The heavy and divers demands, which will be made on a man, have often caused the staff disquiet as a student left college, lest, able though he might be in some areas of ministry, the total demand would over-whelm him. Little surprise then that talk about lay ministry has abounded and that 'time and talents' schemes and lay training ventures have been used to release 'God's Frozen People'. Still, however, it is too often the case that laity are only allowed to 'help the vicar'. Delegation is the keyword. Far more significant are the instances where lay people are enabled to discover their ministry, and so to contribute fresh gifts and insights to the work of the church. The Order of Teachers provided such an opportunity and one has experi-enced others. Another formative influence was the participa-tion of my family in an extended community based on the Franciscan movement. Like so many similar small group and community ventures, we were able to discover a new depth in Christian discipleship through relating to one another and to God, and to discern as our life developed, the complementary gifts within the group, which together made us the Body of Christ. In such small group situations, real sharing becomes possible, the individual becomes valued by the group, and the resources for mission can be harnessed.

It has not been easy to be self-conscious about the stages by which one's understanding of the ministry has advanced. The dramatic contrast between the earliest understanding and that held today is easier to register than each step, which was inevitably largely unconscious. Early questioning of the role expected and a certain discontent with one's capacity to fulfil expectation, the subsequent discovery of the value of shared ministry and of divers patterns of activity at college, and a growing awareness of the tremendous potential in lay minis-try were all important. At the same time, these ideas were being reinforced through a day-to-day experience of the wider church, for Wells was trying to meet another need of the church, that of in-service training for the clergy. In 1967, the 'Refresher Course' began, offering a six- to eight-week course to clergy from many dioceses and, indeed, many coun-tries. Working with small groups of three or four each term, one was made aware of the tremendous pressures on the parochial priesthood, and of the need for clergy to share their responsibility and find support in maintaining vision and mission. The growing demand for proper in-service training programmes in the church has echoed this need, and a visit to

America and participation in an international conference on Ministry and Training made me aware that developments in ministry in England are not an isolated instance.[2] Important though all these individual influences were, the single most important factor was the growing consciousness amongst the staffs of theological colleges of their role as educators.

Of course, they have always been educators, but the secular developments in educational philosophy, which have marked the last ten to fifteen years, have had their effect on theological education as well. Increasingly, college staffs have—as a quick look at the subjects dealt with at the annual meeting makes clear—been made aware of the need for aims and objectives in education, and of the need to determine the content and direction of their courses by those aims.[3] Time and again, the question has been asked—'What are we training men for?' It has been less and less possible to take the answer to this question for granted, and more and more necessary to worry away at it, and allow the conclusion to govern the way you teach and train the ordinands. Yet this process has its other side too, for developing ideas about ministry cannot be treated in isolation from the church's tradition. Thus the educator is caught up in an important process which is inevitably formative for his understanding of ministry. A student of history, and particularly of the history of doctrine, becomes aware of the developments which mark different stages in the church's life and which are the result of the response to the pressures on the church at a given moment. Whether it be Wesley's poor preachers, the fourfold ministry of Calvin or the coming of the Friars, the church's ministry develops forms and functions which are dictated by the inadequacy of ministry in their own day, and a new zeal and vision. New though such developments may be, they none the less have a biblical view of ministry. No doubt, in my

[2] An Ecumenical and International Conference held at Windsor in October 1975, considered ordination training in the wider context of adult education, lay training and in-service training. Some material was subsequently published as *The Educational Role of Theological Colleges and Seminars* (ACCM Occasional Paper No. 6)

[3] In 1969, the main subject was, 'Patterns of Ministry'; in 1971, 'Educational Methods'; in 1972, 'The Aims and Objectives of Training Men and Women for Ministry'.

own case, the study of the Bible and especially of the Old Testament has been a considerable influence on my views on ministry.

The Old Testament may be approached from a number of directions. Contemporary critical scholarship draws our attention away from history and towards the aims of the writers; away from particular texts and narratives and towards a general view of the material. Following this lead, it is possible to see this very divers body of literature as the record of theological thought in Israel over nearly a thousand years, as she sought to understand God, his purpose for the world and her role within it. It is also possible to become aware of the changing patterns of religious belief and practice through the period, forming a precedent for necessary change in our own day. Treated as the continuous record of the community's thought, the material tells us a great deal, explicitly and implicitly about the nature of a religious community. From it we can see how such a community needs to be bound together by a common vision—a common sense of destiny and purpose. The relevance of this vision, and its implications, must be made clear in each generation, and there are those within the community whose job this is. Deviations from the true vision must be corrected, and there are those whom God calls to carry out this vital role. The achievement of God's purpose relies on the co-operative effort of the whole community. The establishment of a quality of life which challenges others, the preservation of justice and the care of the poor are the responsibility of all, if 'all nations will ask to be blessed as you are blessed' (Gen. 12:3). Nevertheless king and judge, seer, prophet and priest exercise particular ministries towards the people and when they fail there is no justice and no 'knowledge of God in the land'. Within this overall pattern, changes in ministry can also be traced, to meet new situations, as for example in the developing and changing function of the prophet. Thus the study of the Old Testament may give us further confidence in assessing the appropriate pattern of ministry for our own day.

The Ministry Today

To this assessment, we must now turn. More recently, I have shared responsibility for the promotion of the Auxiliary ministry and the exploration of other new forms of ministry in the church. From 1974 onwards, the college at Salisbury offered a three-year non-residential training course for those seeking ordination but retaining their secular jobs. With limited time available for training, the need to define this ministry carefully, and to create training priorities in the light of that definition, made a careful appraisal of ministry today imperative. Moving to a diocesan role in theological education, with particular responsibility for Readers, has made this appraisal equally necessary. Indeed one finds that what is, in part, a theoretical exploration at college is vitally practical in a diocese, which like so many others is trying to rationalize ministry in the church of the 80s. The brief recently given to a working party on ministry makes this clear enough—'this Diocesan Synod welcomes the signs of new ministries and asks . . . the working party . . . to identify emerging patterns and to consider what further developments in ministry are necessary to sustain the life and mission of the church'.[4] The resolution implies, as has also been hinted above that there is room for improving change. The Established Church in England has held for many years that the key to effective ministry lies in the parish system. This is the idea that one man or one man and his assistants should minister to a gathered community in a limited geographical area, with a responsibility for all the life within that area. The system has worked well and still has immense value, but its effectiveness is being questioned today and already there are signs of change. It is not easy to make a full appraisal of the effectiveness of parochial ministry. One has to deal with upwards of 12,000 clergy operating in an immense variety of situations. It will however be worth looking at a number of factors, whilst recognizing that they could be added to, under the three headings of—availability, quality and suitability.

Availability has always been an important mark of the Anglican clergyman. He must be available to any person, for whatever purpose, at any time. Today this is made extremely

---

[4] This brief was given by the Diocesan Synod of Lichfield through the Bishop's Council. The brief given to a similar working party in the Diocese of Exeter read: 'To consider how an effective ministry to the parishes of the Diocese can be maintained in the future, in view of the anticipated reductions in the number of full-time clergy available, and the extent to which auxiliary ministry should be employed.'

difficult for a number of reasons. Urbanization is still the most obvious of these. Broadly speaking, because of the parochial system, the people are in the towns and Anglican clergy are in the country. Following the 'Sheffield Report' of 1975 (GS 205), the House of Bishops issued an amended version in 1976 which attempts to redeploy the clergy by 1981, moving them more towards the north and the south-east. Some rural dioceses such as Bath and Wells, Gloucester and Exeter are being asked to lose men. More urban dioceses such as Lichfield, Manchester, Chelmsford and Sheffield may hope to gain some. Such a redeployment is not before time, since it will begin to remedy a situation in which ministry has been seriously impoverished in areas of high population. At the local level, the redistribution is being effected by a system of pastoral reorganization which groups parishes together, and places larger geographical areas under a team of clergy. The net result raises problems for local Christian communities, particularly in rural areas, where a clergyman must now be shared. Redistribution, therefore, increases the effectiveness of the ordained ministry in urban areas, but *numerical strength* is still a problem. As already mentioned, vocations to the ordained ministry have dropped in all churches during the last fifteen years. Since their average age lies in the mid-fifties, the drop in the number of Anglican clergy each year due to death and retirement is greater than the number being ordained. In 1973 there were 13,105 full-time diocesan clergymen, by 1975 that figure had dropped to 12,329 and it has been predicted that it could fall well below 11,000 by 1980. Although, because of reorganization, this does not mean that there are hundreds of jobs going in the Church of England, it does mean that there is a shortage of men to maintain anything like the traditional parochial pattern in England. At the same time there is an *economic* factor to be borne in mind. Even if vocations were forthcoming and there was a substantial increase in the number of parochial clergy, it is doubtful whether the church could meet the bill. During the last decade, the Church Commissioners have made immense efforts to rationalize clergy stipends and make them realistic. Seldom is tribute paid to the very important work done in this area and in that of pensions for clergy. Nevertheless the Commissioners are now clear that any further improvement will have to come from lay giving. Although it must be recognized that few of us give sacrificially, the laity already meet heavy bills to maintain old buildings and meet diocesan quotas, when many would prefer to support the charities and the need for world aid. It is difficult to avoid the conclusion that if the ordained ministry of the church is to be made more available, it will have to be done at minimal cost.

When we turn to the *quality* of ministry, we are again faced with a difficult task as there is a need to speak in general terms of so large a group of men. Whereas once the clergy were largely graduate, this is thankfully so no longer and people come from a wider variety of backgrounds and, indeed, increasingly with considerable experience in another job first. This is an undoubted strength to the ministry, but equally raises questions about the capacity of priests to meet all the varied demands made upon them. Although the pattern is beginning to change, these demands must be met by the individual, largely in isolation, without the real support of other clergy, or of lay groups. There has been within the church no really adequate system of answerability, and with declining numbers of committed lay people who in many cases share some of the present anxiety and bewilderment over trends in belief and practice, it is no wonder that many feel ineffective. Role-definition is a contributory factor too. So many are moved towards ordination by a feeling of compassion and a desire to serve their fellow men, and yet they find the welfare state answering people's needs and fewer knocks coming on the vicarage door. Small wonder, perhaps, that loneliness and strain are marks of the priesthood, and that so many seem to lack real zeal and vision. The demand to redefine the thrust of ministry may be just too much, yet it may be necessary if they are to meet the needs of those to whom they minister.

The *suitability* of the ministry offered is a third area for concern. It can be argued that the characteristic life of contemporary man demands a more sophisticated form of ministry than that traditionally associated with the parish. It is a fairly gifted person who can adequately meet the demands on him as pastor, preacher, teacher, prophet, leader of worship, administrator, etc., and also that he should be a man of prayer. But today's society makes the job even harder. It is to begin with *mobile and fragmented*. Estimates vary as to how often people move, but anyone who has worked in an area of residential estates knows that the turnover of houses can be pretty high. The general movements associated with social change, and the pressure to move to maintain employment, make the parish unit less static than it has ever been. Beyond this, however, man experiences life in several areas. He lives in one place, works in a second, finds recreation in a third and education in a fourth. In all these areas, he belongs to a group of people with whom he shares an important part of his life, and develops independent structures. Unless we are to assume that the church can minister to man in his fragmented experience from the fixed point of the parish, then mobility and fragmentation seriously hinder the effectiveness of the parochial ministry, if it is to be 'ministry to the whole man'. It is possible to raise further questions about the suitability of the traditional view of the parochial ministry, when we turn to a consideration of the basic nature of *the man to whom we minister*. The last 100 years have seen immense strides in the advance of our understanding of man, to which many would say the churches have been slow to react. This affects our capacity to proclaim salvation. First, because many of the images and much of the language which we traditionally employ have little immediate relevance for modern man. Secondly, because our proclamation is insufficiently sensitive to the plight of man, circumscribed as he is by the structures of life, which direct his behaviour. These are vast and important considerations which cannot be dealt with in a paragraph, but it should not go unnoticed that, for example, life after death is of less concern when there is a long life expectation; that sin and repentance have less impact on a generation which questions culpability; and that a certain ambiguity about prayer and the activity of God is inevitable in a scientific and technological age. These are cited not to suggest that they are theological ideas which can be lightly discarded, but that a church which is to be effectively proclaiming salvation needs to attend carefully to the way in which this is done. At the very least we need to recognize that more than ever today the work of the church's theologians needs to be harnessed so that it can inform lay people, who are themselves best suited to proclaim salvation within their particular environment, to individuals and to structures. Surely this must be a key concern for parochial clergy, albeit a demanding one. Again, it seems generally agreed that man, being interdependent on his fellow, finds his fullest maturity within a small group where confidence and mutual trust can grow. If this is the case, then parochial ministry faces yet further demands in terms of developing group life, at depth, within the parish and so further enabling lay people to become equipped to proclaim salvation in contemporary terms. It is surely very important to ask whether the parochial ministry, as it is traditionally understood, can meet all these demands, and difficult to avoid the conclusion that we need a wider view of ministry.

Signs of New Life
Although we have spent some time looking at the severe problems faced by the parochial priesthood, there have been some developments in the last few years, which have helped the situation enormously. Experience through the theological college, as at the Elephant and Castle, and in the wider church has made me aware of great changes in the pattern of church life to meet a changing situation. There are inner city churches where more than half the building has been tastefully converted to provide facilities for sections of society in the area. Others have developed bars and clubs in their extensive basements, which might horrify former incumbents, but enable real contact with a society otherwise largely alienated from the church. There is new interest in co-operating with the movements for good within society, which may have a secular origin such as the aftercare of prisoners, rather than assuming that church-based societies are the only way to proclaim salvation. There is a new awareness, particularly in some of our cathedrals, that the promotion of art and music and much else that ameliorates society's life, is an obligation on the Christian community which would serve the society in which it lives. The great majority of these result from the initiative and imagination of the clergy and the co-operative support of the laity, and they go some way to promote a ministry of the church, which is more suited to contemporary man and provides a platform from which to draw him into relationship with God. As in much else, less dramatic but equally significant, like the effect of the charismatic movement and of a policy of education and development in the

parish, these changes have implications for the ministry to the church too, and here we can list a number of important developments.

There is first the move towards *teams and groups*. These are slightly different. A team ministry brings together a number of people, under a 'Team Rector', who minister to a large area. Although each 'Team Vicar' may have special responsibility for a limited geographical area, specialist gifts can be recognized, and a team will often include someone specializing in youth work or education, for example. Normally there is a Church Council, which is a large and somewhat unwieldy body of lay people representing the whole area. Group ministries are founded by bringing together several parishes, or erstwhile independent geographical areas, which retain a lot of their autonomy, each area maintaining its own council. The clergy work together as far as possible as equals, but without any notable specialization. Both systems tend to break down the isolation of the priest, promoting the opportunity for mutual help, support and sharing. Although many such ventures got off to a shaky start, the second phase of this movement, as pastoral reorganization takes effect, gives grounds for considerable optimism that the parochial ministry is developing in an imaginative and potentially enriching direction. Although it is asking for some sacrifice from priest and people alike, with careful planning, attention to needs and resources and sensitivity to the social character of the area, teams and groups will surely improve the quality of the ministry to the church, and so of the church to the world. This shared responsibility and flexible leadership provides some hope that other forms of ministry may now gain greater acceptance and recognition, and find an integrated position within the church's pattern of ministry. Thus, for example, the closer association of clergy makes more sense of the development of *specialist* and *sector* ministries. We are well used to Hospital and Forces' chaplains, and these specialist ministries have been joined recently by many with entirely new roles. Ministers are being appointed to large commercial organizations, to shopping centres and to other particular areas of society's life. Once again this is an important way in which ministry is developing in a manner likely to increase its effectiveness. The fact that such people can now easily become closely associated with local groups of clergy must further enrich their ministry and much the same could be said about the development of APM.

It is exciting to note the increasing number of men being ordained after training during, and beyond, which they retain secular employment. Whether they are called Auxiliary Pastoral Ministers, Non-Stipendiary Ministers, Honorary Ministers or Self-supporting Ministers, the last five years has seen a lot of debate about this development. Indeed it has been the need to define this ministry which has prompted a lot of the wider debate about ministry. The movement finds its origin in two separate developments. The *worker-priest* movement took many forms in England and on the continent but was essentially a move to ordain men to a priesthood, which had no necessary links with the parochial system, and developed ministry in the working part of man's life. The *Auxiliary Parochial Ministry* began as a movement to develop an assistant ministry in the parishes. Although, thus, developing independently of one another, the difference between them in England today is somewhat indistinct and no one view of this ministry prevails. Some attention will be given to this below, since there is an understanding of it which goes a long way to meet some of the problems for ministry already outlined. At the moment, there are those within the APM fold who see their ministry largely in parochial terms, and those who are keen to discover a ministry at work, and it is generally agreed that one cannot be a priest in only one part of one's life. 'APM's are therefore another growth-point in the ministry, even if their precise role needs some clarification. Significant too, and really part of this movement, is the *Retirement Ministry*. This term has been abandoned centrally by the church, but with earlier retirement on better pensions, an increasing number of men are training for ordination in their late fifties and being ordained to an assistant role in the parish in which they live. Such men could go some way to meeting the problem raised by pastoral reorganization and may reasonably anticipate ten to fifteen years of lively service in the ministry.

At the same time, the need for a local figure is being explored in terms of a *Local Ministry*. In a number of churches, Elders are being appointed with special responsibility, particularly in pastoral work, but also sometimes sharing overall responsibility with the incumbent for the ministry of the church in local society. Once again, the movement takes many forms. In some parishes an Eldership Scheme embodies simply teams of visitors, in others the Elders are the incumbent, a curate, a Reader and perhaps the Churchwardens. Such schemes share a common aim in wishing to involve in a recognizable way the natural leadership of the Christian community, to develop genuine lay ministry and to meet the growing needs of the church, which the parish priest can barely do. It is convenient to bring in the *Readers* movement as part of this local ministry. Readers are well established, and although undervalued and often underemployed, yet still make a lively contribution to the church's ministry. Recently expanded to include women, it is probably true to say that the full potential of this movement has not been realized. Readers have become floating office-takers and preachers, and been largely excluded from a full share in the ministry to the church. Recent revision of their training, a new interest in local ministry and the lively openness of a number of those at present in training all suggest that here, too, there is potentially new life in the ministry.

Finally, in looking at signs of life in the ministry, further mention must be made of *lay ministry*. There is, as has been mentioned above, a new interest amongst lay people in being better equipped to play their part in the total ministry of the church. Many dioceses are developing extensive courses to meet this need. The aim is that those who already exercise ministry within the church as group leaders, Sunday school teachers, and a hundred and one other tasks, should do their work more competently and confidently. Yet for many, their involvement in study and training is simply in order that they may play a more effective part in the work of the church in the world. It is of course tempting to ask whether some of these people should really come within the categories already described. Should they be recognized in some way, licensed or even ordained? Nowhere is this a more crucial question than in the area of women's ministry. The fact that women have not been eligible for ordination to the priesthood in the Church of England in the past, inevitably focuses our attention on this question today. However it may be that in the light of the diversity within the present pattern of ministry, we should ask first what sort of ministry does the church need, and then where does ordination of male or female fit in.

The answer is not clear. There are several very pressing matters requiring definition and clarification before there can, once again, be a church view of ministry. There is, for example, dispute over the relative status of the APM and the Reader. The latter can easily be seen as an office-taker, the former can be treated as a mass-priest. The more one emphasizes that no liturgical function can be properly undertaken outside the context of a wider ministry to the community, the difference between the two diminishes. Again one must ask if an APM and a Worker-Priest are really distinct. Can one be a priest in only part of one's life? Others would want to question the advisability of training men for priesthood in secular occupations, as it further inhibits genuine lay responsibility for ministry in the world. Some will want to question the notion that we can adequately train men for priesthood in a three-year non-residential course. Others will want to stress that there must be no hint that we are developing a second-class priesthood in the APM. Sooner or later, in every debate on the subject of ministry, questions like these, and there are many others, lead us back to the need to define the central terms ministry, priesthood and ordination. At the beginning of this essay, I indicated how my own understanding of ministry had changed after fifteen years in three particular ways. Time spent in a parish, in a theological college from which I developed wide responsibilities, and latterly in a diocesan role in theological education, has led to this change. It has been possible to observe and experience something of the inadequacy and yet the potential in the church's present ministry. It is a bold person who would attempt a guess at the developments of the next ten years, particularly when there are so many unanswered questions. Yet it is vital to ask what sort of ministry will be needed to equip and to serve a church, increasingly subject to organizational change, rediscovering the value of small group life, disrupted by mobility and the fragmented experience of life, and recognizing that mission is the responsibility of the whole people of God, and is a mission to individuals, to communities and to structures.

A Ministry for the Future

Remembering that we are talking about the ministry *to* the church, the ministry which will 'equip the saints', it will be first a group ministry. The days of isolation, of one man and his people, are nearly over. If there are disadvantages in terms of the loss of the individual with whom a community can identify, there are compensating advantages in the support to be found within a group and, with sensitive leadership, in the genuine *complementarity* of ministry which makes full use of the resources available. At the helm and heart of the group will be the parochial priesthood. However we define the area of responsibility of such a group, it is bound to have geographical boundaries and the parish priest will still need to relate to all or part of such an area. New emphases in their ministry will however become apparent, for they will need the ability to enable a group to work; the maturity to discern not only the strengths and weaknesses of others, but of themselves; the wisdom to integrate a group of people who are diverse in function but complementary in nature. Such ministers will need to be trained as fully as the church knows how, and will be wholly employed by her. They will be joined in the group by a number of people, exercising a variety of functions and so *sharing ministry*. Some of them, but not all, will be ordained. Important among these will be the APM or *Non-Stipendiary Ministers*, undertaking a highly significant ministry, which finds its centre in work and other areas of man's life from which the parochial minister is largely excluded. Not only will they exercise a full ministerial function in this situation, they will also, importantly, bring their insights and expertise into the ministerial group, and so play a complementary role, which if given full force will further enable ministry to the whole man. Since clearly specialist and sector ministers are suited to make a somewhat parallel contribution, this very particular view of APM requires some justification.

As hinted earlier, there are problems when it comes to agreed definitions of ordination, priesthood and ministry. The primary model for ministry must always be Jesus Christ himself. In so far as Jesus had a ministry to all men, the church, as the body of Christ, shares that ministry now amongst all its members. Yet we know that Jesus spent much time in prayer, that he worshipped and studied the scriptures, that he equipped himself, that is to say, for ministry. He equipped his disciples too and the process was continued in the Early Church. So, together, Christians today exercise a ministry *to* the church whenever through pastoral care, through patient explanation of the scriptures, through the leading of worship, etc., they enable their fellows to be more effective workers for God. Yet beyond this ministry to the church in which we all share, there has always been a more extended ministry, hitherto identified largely in the ordained priesthood, which has both a representative and an enabling aspect. Ordination recognizes that a person has been called by God to represent Him to the people and the people to Him—to share in the mediation of Christ himself. Ordination also gives a person recognition as having God's authority to enable the church to carry out His purpose, through a variety of functions. Amongst these functions and surely central amongst them are the celebration of the eucharist and the pronouncement of absolution. Where these criteria are being satisfied, ordination to priesthood would seem to be appropriate

The APM exercising ministry at work would seem to me to so satisfy them. He will exercise a *representing* function, because he will identify Christian presence in the situation, in the same way that the parish priest does in the parish. Thus the minister becomes a sign of the church's involvement in this aspect of man's life. He expresses God's concern for the people and becomes an important focus for other Christians sharing in the situation. Such a person will also be an *enabler*. He will be trained to catalyse confident Christian witness and action, again precisely as in the parochial sphere. This will be done by playing a part in the theological education of Christians in their work; by discerning the body of Christ, as other Christians are identified and enabled to grow through mutual support. A third role, for which training should fit him, will be the theological interpretation and prophetic challenge of the structures and purpose of working life. Lastly, he will be available, as any other priest, as a pastor and leader of worship. In all this such people have the great advantage over specialist and sector ministers, whose work they will also complement, that they are thoroughly conversant with and immersed in a significant area of man's fragmented life. In the parish, in addition to sharing with the staff group, one would expect such people to make their contribution in the particular fields for which their talents suit them, with only limited time available. Thus they might be used as teachers, evangelists, pastors or liturgists and so a group of them would, together, exercise a wide ministry to the church.

At a third level in the group, we may expect to find the *local ministers*. The Reader is the nearest example of this at the moment, but the movement towards Elders may be a clearer indication of what will develop. Because of the diversity which already exists in respect of Elders, it will be necessary to reserve the title for those who clearly exercise ministry to the church beyond the level of that of the committed layman. Where it can be shown that there is a shared responsibility for the life and work of the church community, so that the person is a point of reference and enables the church to function, such a distinction may perhaps be seen to be made. Once again because of the pressure of time, their diversity of function and their complementarity will be important. Their presence within the shared ministry of the group will be a significant way of ensuring adequate ministry, particularly in isolated rural areas, but if group life within the church receives the attention, which it should in the future, then here too they will be increasingly important. If only because of the liturgical needs of the church, I would expect a number of them to be ordained, and providing the criteria above are met, this would seem appropriate. Having defined the need and the ministry which could answer it, there can be no reason why ordination should not be applied to men and women alike within the group. It will, however, be important that not all are ordained. There is no obvious need for the teacher, for example, to be ordained rather than licensed. Nevertheless if they are not to be ordained licensing will be important, if some order is to be maintained in what will be a rather fluid situation, and great care will have to be exercised in moving from place to place in these days of mobility.

Order may be further maintained, I suggest, by the demands of training. Ministry like teaching is a gift, but it can be embellished by good training. More and more dioceses are setting up lay training courses, and we shall, I believe, see a move towards the full integration of ministry and training. In one diocese there is now a standard two-year course of study for all lay people. Entitled 'What is a Christian?'[5] its aim is to equip lay people for confident expression of their faith. An Introduction to the Bible and to the Church in history is followed by an exploration of belief and behaviour. By following this course and adding a third year of study and some weekend training, men and women can qualify for Readership, and in future perhaps for Eldership or Local Ministry. Some may discover a vocation for APM or parochial ministry, and their basic training would then count towards training for these ministries. In this way an attention to the need to equip lay people for their ministry to the world will inevitably lead to some discovering a more particular ministry to the church, and it should perhaps be the case that the community will ask some to prepare for this. No longer then need we rely wholly on individuals experiencing a call in the traditional way, but may hope that God will use fellow men and women to discern where ministry lies. It is in such small but profound ways that we give reality to the notion that we are engaged in a common task to fulfil God's purpose; that we are, together, the Body of Christ, and everyone, members one of another.

An age ago, or so it seems, the ministry of the church meant a personal call to ordained priesthood. Today that ministry stands at something of a crossroads. There are a lot of questions still unanswered, but the signs are there, for the discerning, that the church is rediscovering her purpose once again, a purpose which involves the whole people of God. Signs too that the need to be equipped for this purpose can be met, if she will obey the prompting of the spirit, and play a part in calling men and women to a shared ministry to the church—a ministry which embraces many people with different and complementary gifts. There may be some disorder for a time. The pattern of ministry, which eventually transpires, may be unfamiliar, even alarming to some. Yet the Spirit of God has never stood still, and faith is not about security through particular structures, but security through trust. The question is will we trust God and learn from another as we discover a new vision together of ministry and mission?

[5] The two-year course has been written and developed by the Dioceses of Salisbury and Lichfield. It leads to a Bishop's Certificate in Christian Education. Several other dioceses are beginning to operate the scheme and further information can be obtained from The Council for Ministry, Church House, Crane Street, Salisbury.

6

On Ministry and Ordination

Ruth Matthews

Ruth Matthews was born on a farm in Kent; she still retains a passionate bigotry in matters of fruit, cricket, and Canterbury Cathedral.

She came to theology from history and a short period working in the Cathedral Library. If she had not been a minister she would have liked to be an archivist. After training for the Baptist ministry at Regent's Park College, Oxford, she had a pastorate for two years. She is married to a Baptist minister; they have two boys whose religion is 'based more on steam and model railways'. She is at present a member of the team ministry of the Central Church, Swindon, an Area of Ecumenical Experiment.

My Christian experience has deep roots in the Baptist tradition, going back in one part of my family for several generations of determined dissent. The involvement of my immediate family in the local church, and in wider denominational service, meant that I grew up knowing the strengths and weaknesses of at least our part of the Christian church. My basic picture of the church, its work and its mission and the place of the ordained ministry within it still stands—with, I hope, a widening and a deepening of understanding as the years pass.

When I came to feel that I should myself enter the ministry I was happy to do so within the Baptist tradition, though by now very aware of the other branches of the church. I suppose that I based my ideas of the way I would actually work on what I had seen other ministers do. Theologically I held the view that to be ordained was to be set apart by the church for particular work which I would be doing: playing a certain part in the life of the body. Ordination was not conferring any status for life, nor any gifts in a different way from that which God enabled people to do any other piece of his work.

It seemed more of a responsibility than a privilege, more of a necessity, than something to get excited about. It was, for me, of the daily bread of the church in a way which did not encourage me perhaps enough to idealism and vision.

This low-key picture chimed with some of the questions that were being raised when I was at college during my training, to produce not now so much a dull sound as a discord! During the summer of 1964 when I left college and prepared for ordination I could muster little enthusiasm for the work I was about to do. (Don Camillo-type conversations took place: 'Lord, don't You think I might have made a

TEOO—5 **

mistake about this—or could I venture to suggest You might even be wrong?'. . . 'Wait and see'. . . So I waited—and in the end perhaps I shall see.)

It was a time when question after question was being raised about the relevance of the church, the role of the minister and the ways of formulating faith today. We were still in the wake of all that *Honest to God* had let loose—and we had a lot of academic theology and very little experience to use in coping with it.

During the first years of my ministry these questions continued to live not only in my mind but in the religious press of the time. The journal *New Christian* published articles and letters which I think spoke to many of my generation—some of whom moved out of the ministry in their quest. Letters were printed with comments like this: 'What relevance has a priest to the Christian faith? What am I doing in this job at all. . . . In an area of very low religious practice, it was hard to avoid the feeling that you could either wear yourself out with non-stop visiting, or else you could sit at home and do the crossword and the world would be apparently no different.'[1] Another letter comments on an article: 'G. H. claims that unlike the twenty-plus the forty-plus have adapted themselves successfully to the difficulties of being a parish priest. But to this claim the twenty-plus may well reply: Yes, but at what a price! . . . the twenty-plus may be desperately frightened of being forced into the same mould.'[2]

It felt as if very few older ministers had noticed how much the world around the church had changed in the last hundred years. If they had, they told us either that we had to stand our ground and not give in, or, for young ministers without many resources of our own, we were presented with rather grand Abrahamic demands to go out, not knowing where. This easily resulted in a mixture of apprehension and confusion which led sometimes to creeping paralysis rather than adventurous steps forward.

At meetings of ministers' fraternals and other clerical gatherings I recall feeling that I was not one of them—and did not want to be! This was a period when there was (I think for the first time), a real decline in the number of ordinands in all

[1] *New Christian,* 10 March 1966
[2] *New Christian,* 5 May, 1966

churches, and a time too when some ordained men were leaving the ministry—or at least leaving the 'normal' sphere of ministry, the local church or parish. Many became over-defensive, too, about how hard they worked, as if to make up for the fact that half the time they weren't sure how much it really mattered. Some younger ministers felt that although their work had a kind of intrinsic spiritual importance, they still did not have what they described as a 'man-sized job'.

There was in this a grappling with the fact that in many ways the ministry had lost a lot of ground in terms of status and pay in relation to other professional jobs, and in the way the work was viewed both by Christians and non-Christians. It was easy to say that of course status doesn't matter and indeed is wrong for a minister of the gospel—and we all kept saying so, for this was the time when the 'servant church' was a favourite sub-ject—but in fact it didn't help morale which was already at a low ebb. Instead of being looked up to in subtle ways in the community we were being pressed to defend and define our role, with our backs against the crumbling church wall.

This was the background to ordination when it is said: 'She is being ordained to preach and teach the word of God from the Holy Scriptures, to lead the worship of the church and administer the Sacraments of Baptism and the Lord's Supper, to be a faithful shepherd of the flock of Christ and to do the work of an evangelist.'[3] This, being interpreted, seemed to mean that you were to organize and undertake all the worship on Sundays (as a kind of solo performance, with particular emphasis on a strong and twenty-minute sermon), any kind of prayer meetings, Bible studies during the week—to prepare candidates for church membership, and to oversee the work of junior church or Sunday school; and under the heading (presumably) of being a faithful shepherd you should chair every conceivable committee, speak often to the women's meeting or sisterhood, run the youth club if necessary, and, above all, visit, visit, visit—especially the flock and after them all the pagans you could find at home willing to receive you. It wasn't a bad thing if the minister took a lead in the town,

[3] 'The Ordination of a Minister', Ernest Payne and Stephen Winward, *Orders and Prayers for Church Worship,* Carey Kingsgate, 1960

village or estate—providing it was about the 'right' things—and providing it didn't stop her doing any of the real work. The congregation would get restive about that brave minister who dared to publish his various civic involvements in the church magazine, and ask him if he was sure he still had time for his 'proper work'. The interpretation of the ordination statement was inviolate and absolute.

What is more, in a Baptist church, the local congregation is entirely responsible for all the salary of that particular minister and this makes the minister 'theirs' in a way which has many dangers. It also creates a position of some isolation. Baptist churches are independent of each other and of any central structure. They are bound together only by ties of fellowship. The Baptist Union is a voluntary federation of churches, not a Church. The people in the central offices and the superintendents, who have pastoral responsibilities over an area, are there for encouragement, advice, exhortation; to co-ordinate certain areas of work, and order those things best done on a national or regional basis, but they have no authority. This lies with the local church meeting of each church. In practice a lot of the 'guidelines' are followed quite happily as a norm but there is no 'must' from anyone outside the church meeting. This has always encouraged independence of mind and judgement, a healthy use of all the parts of the 'body' as it is locally encountered, and a chance for gifts of the Spirit to flower. At its best, it promotes responsible decision-making by the whole people of God and an experience of close fellowship and concern, coupled with an emphasis on the individual, his or her response to God in Jesus Christ and commitment to God's work. At its worst, it degenerates into mere eccentricity, domination by cliques, lack of responsibility or fellowship with the church catholic, and a feeling of strait-jacketed isolation for the minister.

However, in the average church the Baptist tradition of the functional nature of the ministry did give some confidence in the role crisis. We all knew that full-time, set-apart ministers only happened as congregations grew larger and decided to set free one member from earning his living to do the work which was the work of them all. This meant that when others wrote: 'Many young clergy are realizing that in an ideal church they would be redundant' we knew perfectly well that the ideal was rather more eschatological than was so easily assumed!

The other confidence-booster for Baptist ministers was the fact that they are very definitely 'called' to particular churches; if a church does not feel it is right for him to come, it will not have him. Because lay leadership is generally strong, churches will go for two years, if necessary, looking for the right person. They may well thankfully throw everything at him when he arrives, but, on the whole, he knows that he and they agree on his coming to that particular place. There are many drawbacks to this system, but at a time of confusion over whether you as a minister are necessary (and at a time for me personally when there was the added pressure of being one of the few women ministers in the denomination) it can be helpful to know that one church does definitely want you.

Over the years since I was ordained the 'role crisis' seems to have receded into the background. Perhaps it is because people have come to terms with the insecurity, the fact of setting out, not knowing where you are to go. Partly it is due to the working out of more flexible patterns of ministry, and a wider understanding of ministry among congregations. People hanker after the days when the minister used to visit them once a month for a friendly chat, but they no longer believe that that is all they are paying him for. Many are glad to see ministers experimenting in forms of industrial or commercial chaplaincy, for example, as representing the whole church. For whatever reason, ministers seem to be more confident in carving out their role, less bothered by the nonstructured nature of the job. For myself, I am no more able to define my role (in precise non-ordination vow ways) than I used to be, but I find it quite appropriate to live like this!

One book and one article were helpful in this context. Stephen MacKie's book, *Patterns of Ministry,* had some very useful chapters. He talks about the growth of specialist forms of ministry and in dealing with this shows how these challenge the churches to rethink and restate their doctrine of the ministry. A long quotation is necessary to show the way in which this book was helping some of us to think through a proper application of those ordination vows.

'They [specialist ministers] would consider that their work lay at the growing points of society, in a way that the work of the minister in the traditional rural or suburban parish no longer does (the minister in the inner city or in a new housing area is in a different case). They would consider their ministry as directed to all who with them stood at that particular frontier of society and not just to the faithful Christians there. Certainly one of their tasks is to form Christian congregations, but to form them for mission, rather than to cherish them.

'In a sense this is to return to an older view of the pastoral ministry, the view which saw the parish minister as the one who, in a particular place, was responsible for making clear the Word of God to every man, and for interpreting that Word in terms of the pressures and structures of society. We have seen how, in great measure, this view has been replaced by another, in which the professional minister is the leader (or functionary) of a Christian congregation. This process was the inevitable result of social change. What some would say is that this remains the task of the Church, but a task which must now be fulfilled in a different way and at different points.' [4]

The minister to be at the 'growing points of society', the forming of congregations for mission within that society, and especially the minister as 'responsible for making clear the Word of God to every man, and for interpreting that Word in terms of the pressures and structures of society'—yes, this is preaching and teaching, but it isn't limited to Sunday services and the Fellowship at 7.30 on Wednesdays. This kind of writing helped to give glimmerings of what we might be about.

The scene is approached from quite a different angle by Monica Furlong, in her book *With Love to the Church*,[5] and in an article which took hold of me at the time, in *New Christian*[6] (also given as a paper to the Wakefield Diocesan Clergy Conference). Passages such as these provided a hopeful and creative alternative to the devalued way in which clergy tended to see themselves: . . . 'the clergy, of course, often act a role, and indeed it is difficult for them to help it, since their parishioner and others often thrust it upon them. But since the clergy stand so uncompromisingly for a belief in

[4] Stephen MacKie, *Patterns of Ministry*, Collins, 1969
[5] Monica Furlong, *With Love to the Church*, Hodder and Stoughton, 1965
[6] Monica Furlong, 'The Parson's Role to-day', *New Christian*, 16 June 1966

love, and since the Christian faith is intangible, and since it is difficult to imagine what the job is if it is not about love, then it is harder for the priest to escape successfully into an act than it is for the social worker.

'At this particular time there is perhaps a strong temptation among some members of the clergy to adopt a social worker act, to take refuge behind one of the comforting and reassuring masks which others in the helping professions are lucky enough to be able to wear. At least these roles are something the world can understand.

'I cannot speak for other laymen, but this is something I deeply regret. . . .

'From here on, I want to suggest, the clergyman's great strength will lie in the fact he has no strength except the strength of love. He is closer to Christ than he has been for centuries because, like Christ, he has so few defences against the world. Where once he kept a stable, hunted twice a week, and had a whole army of servants, he now runs an old car and helps with the washing-up.

'Where once he was the most educated man in his community, along with the doctor and the squire, he is now no better educated than a large number of the population. Where religion was the most important thing in people's lives, it now takes second place to other, more shallow influences.

'Now much of this is stripped away, but with it much that encouraged self-deception.'

Daniel Jenkins, some years earlier, came at the same question: 'It is safe to assume, when a pattern of ministerial behaviour has become conventionalized, familiar and more or less acceptable to the general public of the society in which the minister moves that it represents a measure of secularization. It is a sign that the Church is becoming conformed to this world which passes away.'[7]

There are two places, on a very practical level, where my expectations of ministry have undergone significant and happy changes. The first is the movement towards team ministry. When I left college a Baptist minister might well be in charge of his or her own church or churches but attached to a larger church and a senior minister. This was the situation I was in, and all the signs then were that after this first 'curacy'

[7] Daniel Jenkins, *The Protestant Ministry*, Faber and Faber, 1958

you would have a church of your own. Some people, right from the start, were on their own. In a Baptist church, this would mean 'on your own' as regards relationships with other ministers or other churches; you would, within your own church, be working with the deacons and church meeting. No accountability existed outside the local church, and 'fellowship' was distant (except perhaps in the big urban conurbations), and depended upon how you threw yourself into wider Baptist life: it was an optional extra.

After my first experience of ministry (small churches on a housing estate and in a village, attached to a larger town church), I did go to a 'church of my own' with a difference. A new group ministry was starting. We still had three ministers and three churches, but the links between the churches grew, with joint activity as it was appropriate (they were some distance apart). At the same time the ministers were pledged to all three churches, not just one; each of them accepted each of us as minister. We saw ourselves growing into a team with regular meeting and certain degrees of accountability as well as a responsibility for each other.

Teams and groups of all sorts have been developing over the years. It is now quite normal among all the branches of the church, to belong to team ministries. There is published every year a document *The State of the Teams* based on questionnaires to existing teams. They take many forms, but most of them seem to be a good development both for congregations and ministers.

This brings us to the second of the changes which have been significant for me: the ecumenical movement in the context of the local church, and the growth of ministry not only within a team but within an ecumenical team. That has been the second part of my ministerial experience, and one which I think is reflected generally and is growing. Here you have the benefits of a team ministry pulled out to form a fuller pattern. Problems of isolation are likely to be reduced in any team; in an ecumenical one it is not just personal isolation which is overcome, but also the mental isolation of thinking along one set of tracks. Metaphorically the points which had once been fixed are now movable and you can go from one line to another and find all kinds of interesting and different stations.

Much is now written about team and group ministry and I do not want to add to the theory of this but nevertheless I would like to emphasize its importance through the window of my own (limited) experience.

There is first of all the stimulus that comes from being set down together with people of other traditions and assumptions. It is much less easy to get stale or fixed. It is also more difficult to be lazy or to be overworked when you are all keeping pastoral eyes on each other. It allows for more specialization than would be possible with the 'normal' system, as different people take responsibility for different areas of life in church or in community, while at the same time not being cut off from the continuing everyday life of the ministry. We have been able to do this, especially as in bringing five congregations together we were able (once the initial enormous administrative and pastoral burden had been lifted), to release time and energy through rationalizing the routine work. It means that one person has oversight of all the pastoral work, and another of worship, though all except our industrial chaplain and diocesan/district lay training adviser in the pastoral work share of course in the worship. Others take special responsibility in work with young people, in health and social welfare, in planning and politics, in our links with the world church, and act as 'resource persons' for groups with these concerns within the congregation. A new initiative in commercial chaplaincy in the centre of town has been started. This not only benefits and stretches the people concerned but also the congregation and, we hope, Christian engagement with the world and society around us.

Alongside all that is most obviously creative and helpful it is important to mention the apparent problems. Team life can produce tensions which you would not otherwise encounter and this is painful but not bad. Most ministers were trained to work with a congregation, and have the assumption that even if they are *primus inter pares*, they will certainly be *primus*, trained to be independent, standing on their own feet, taking full responsibility. If in an assistant or curate's position, they would assume that it was only a matter of time before it was their turn to be in charge. All this militates against the development of teams, where you are accountable to other ministers as well as congregations, and where, as co-operation progresses, you may be responsible for one area only, and have to admit in answer to a question 'No, I don't know, you'll have to ask my colleague'. Knowing and co-ordinating every-thing gives you power, and this power you have to surrender in a team. This, at least, is our experience, which we feel to be valuable.

Some teams have a very definite leader and some a small hierarchy. Ours has no official leader. If there had been someone very obviously senior in terms of age or experience it might have happened, but it did not, and we now hold to this as a principle. Each of us leads on the area that is 'theirs' and in small practical matters, after some chaos, we use the simple principle of taking turns on a rota—such matters as chairing the team meeting or being its secretary. But of course there are tensions, and there is a great need for honesty. We have found it very helpful to have a 'consultant' to come in from time to time to help us look at our objectives and as an outsider whom we trust, sometimes to point out both the blocks and the creative points in our working together. We have found that meeting for prayers daily is something we have come to rely on. Ecumenical Teams are helped when it is possible for the mutuality they want to foster to be recognized by the denomi-nations. In dioceses where, for example, mutual recognition of ministries in local ecumenical projects (and through shar-ing agreements) is not as normal as it is in ours, it makes relationships much more difficult.

With the growth of trust and through the way in which you can each build on your own particular gifts, it also becomes possible to acknowledge your weaknesses and in difficult times to be supported by colleagues. One way and another teams do give ministers opportunities for personal growth which they are less likely to have otherwise. We are encour-aged to work at difficult relationships in a way that we might otherwise avoid, and we have to work out what Christian love is within a fairly testing microcosm of the church. We also face the whole area of 'spirituality' together. Very often it has been assumed that the minister is automatically better at praying and responding to God. Again, a minister surely believes everything in the right way and is not thought to have difficulties with the Bible or the creed. Whether a congrega-tion really thinks this or not, a minister hesitates to share doubts or radical reappraisals for fear of worrying them as well as from any fear of heresy charges. Team ministry, when it is working well, can be very helpful in these areas of a minister's life. A team can of course become too much of a little community of its own so that families find them a strain as support, previously found in the family context, gravitates to the team. This needs to be watched, even though there is the compensative advantage that it is always possible to find someone else on duty if the family wants some privacy or 'time off'. Husband and wife colleagues within a team can also provide irritation as well as amusement for other colleagues and both advantages and disadvantages for the couple—more of this later.

Teams also need to watch the new situation created with the congregations involved. Where a minister has worked closely with church council, deacons, elders, or any other local church structure, the team can make church members and especially the officers feel shut out. This danger had been pointed out to us and we are trying to work in a very open fashion as well as developing the team support. In a very practical way we have found, for example, that we must limit 'team' business and be careful that we do not assume certain decisions as made and then put full team weight behind them. We try to make sure that in any area of church life the minister concerned explores matters with the relevant church group, makes the smaller decisions with them and brings the larger ones to the church council, only reporting en route to the team to make sure that there are no breakdowns in communication. These are the kinds of practical question that need to be worked at in order that underneath the day by day trivia we are all partners in the ministry and mission of the church.

It is interesting to me as a Baptist to note that some of the earliest Baptist writings in the seventeenth century show a plurality of ministers in any one congregation. (These would be men of several different working occupations.) John Smyth had argued for a 'college of pastors' but very soon churches in fact moved towards a one-man ministry within the total ministry of each congregation.

When I speak of team ministry, or indeed ministry in any sense, I realize that I am making assumptions which are not shared by all Christians about the participation of women. Since I live and work knowing that I am both ordained and a woman I do make the assumption that this is quite normal. I am reluctant to talk about 'my ministry as a woman' unless others are willing to talk about 'my ministry as a man', but since many do not share my assumptions I ought to say something here about this.

My experience has been that there has been more fuss about whether I would be accepted as a woman than was warranted. There were few enough female Baptist ministers when I was ordained for others still to feel it odd, and for me to feel odd not in the congregation but in the all-male clerical gatherings which I rather disliked. Men covered what was presumably embarrassment by over-reaction and I got very tired of jokes on the subject and of the inevitable address beginning, 'Brethren and Sister . . .', with an accompanying patronizing smile. I over-reacted in return and I continue to do so when I am treated as something peculiar. Perhaps one day I shall grow out of this! Meanwhile, as far as the work was concerned it didn't seem to make any difference, except that it helped to break down barriers very often with the non-Christian.

There are some occasions when people prefer to see a man or a woman pastorally and for this reason I have been glad latterly to be in a 'mixed' team. I have also, since marriage, had a colleague in the ministry as well as a husband. This has the same advantage in that people can choose if they want to talk to a man or a woman. It also had personal advantages for us in that we were very happily invited to share the ministry in one church while we had very small children. They gave us *carte blanche* concerning which of us did what. We did not divide the work according to any traditional male and female role, but more in terms of personality and gifts; in leadership and policy we shared equally. We felt that this gave an added dimension to the work even though it did not give the church any more than one person's time at that point. We felt it was, on the whole, helpful for the children. They always had Mummy or Daddy in terms of their security, and even though one of us tended to be out a lot, it was better balanced than in many clerical households, where children have undiluted mother and a conscientiously absentee father.

Domestically and personally, however, there were strains which were not easy. Practically, in a marriage where you have separate jobs, or where one is primarily in charge of home and children, you do not need to go into details. We always had to have catching-up sessions both on how Mrs Smith was in the hospital and on the nappy situation or where the other one might have put that crucial bit of Lego. You can find that, while you share the same ideas in general, you have to come to terms with details in the way that the other does something quite differently. You can feel threatened by the other, or just irritated! Working together so closely means that work can take over practically every conversation. In all, we found this useful for a few years but would not like to continue it for too long, nor would we have been able to enter in on it, I think, until both of us had had separate experiences. We are now trying, within our group, to separate out our areas of ministry so that the kind of catching up we do should not be more than that between all of us as colleagues. When we move from here we think we may separate out further, though as yet we do not see the next step. It is probably better for a group ministry, too, not to contain both husband and wife, although, being aware of this, we have all worked at it.

The same experience that has been mine in a 'husband and wife' ministry has also been mine within a team: that work is organized according to need, interests, gifts and weaknesses, not according to any understanding of what might be masculine and what feminine. Perhaps we symbolize our awareness of this by the fact that when we are together it is usually the men who end up making the coffee! Yet without there being anything specific or definable from which we could say, 'Ah yes, we do need a woman', there is a growing sense, I think, that a 'mixed team' is what it ought to be. We have at present four men and three women in our team. Two of the women are ordained, and one replaced a man. At the time, with the increase of the female strength, some jokes were made, but now it seems to be very much an accepted part of the order of things. The team would not want to be all-male (nor all-female) and nor would the congregations with whom we work want it to be. Outside the Christian community too, I think it is valuable for this kind of team to be seen working together.

The necessity for the ordination of women is clear to me. What is important is that people should in some sense find God and should be able to work and live in ways that open up the fulness of human life. The Christian church should be the vehicle for this, and in a period when we have generally been self-critical and aware of failings in the church, we still hold on to the fact that treasure may be contained in an earthen vessel, and that the treasure is not dimmed by our failings. We can make it more difficult for people to find, however, and while we are aware of ways in which, being human, we are bound to fail we should not add to them by those which can be avoided.

Many Biblical texts are difficult to interpret: that which tells us that God made man in his image is notoriously so. However, if you take it seriously, you have to grapple with the fact that in this is included the other phrase: 'male and female created he them'. 'In his image . . . male and female.' [8] Yet the traditional ways of speaking about God are very male. Father . . . Lord . . . King; the 'popular image' is a male one. We may say that of course we know that God transcends male and female, that this is only a manner of speaking, or that it would be better to get away from all this anthromorphism and turn to the 'ground of our being'. But I think that because we are human we are likely to go on being anthromorphic about God, and if we do so in these male terms we are depriving ourselves and others of the fulness of God.

There are other images. The Spirit, for example, had a female connotation in Hebrew which has been lost to us. The (female) wisdom of God is a concept lost by Western Christendom. It was not mother church but Jesus himself who would have gathered people like chicks under a mother hen. Julian of Norwich is a mystic who found herself looking at the male-and-female in God in order to express more fully what she believed about His relationship with her.

There may be many who would agree that it is time for a recovery of this aspect of thinking about God; who would agree that language is important, but who want to stop there. Yet it is my conviction that recovery or discovery is impossible if it is not seen as well as heard. It is true that in many ways women have been treated as equals within the Christian church and have played an important part in its life and

[8] Genesis 1:27

mission. Through the work of religious orders on the one hand and the lay preachers and Sunday School teachers on the other, as well as in the increased lay leadership in many branches of the church today, they have been able to participate in ways which have been vital. At various points in history this has happily been far in advance of any secular contribution they could make. This has been seen as part of the freedom that Christ came to give, and as an aspect of his reconciling work.

Yet the female dimension of God, whenever it flowers, seems quickly to be lost or scaled down. As long as men are either the only sex to be ordained or very much the predominant sex (so that women ministers are assumed to be odd) the image of God will basically be male. Jesus in his body had to belong to one sex, as he had to belong to one nation, but the 'body' which we speak of belonging to now may be male and female. As we represent God to one another, as we allow the image of God to be seen in his world, so we must represent him in his fulness as male and female.

This is the inner dimension of the thing. There is also the external fact that ordination has usually been *the* qualification in decision making and policy structures of the church. There is now much more attention given to 'lay participation', and the dissenting churches have continually tried to keep this principle alive, but it is still true that the shape of the church is made by men.

What difference does this make? We do not know, but I suspect it does make a difference. It is difficult, almost impossible, to lay down hard and fast distinctions between men and women. Old assumptions have been challenged and the whole area is under debate. Now that women are educated, have many different kinds of work open to them, have laws passed in favour of equal opportunity, it is seen that they are capable of work which used to be thought impossible. With reliable contraception and a change of social attitudes about a man's role as well (it is gradually more and more possible for a man to push a pram or hang out the washing without comment), there are less obvious differences in the home. We have also learnt that here as well as in other areas of life generalizations are dangerous as well as irritating. 'All women are illogical' takes on the same usefulness as 'all

143

red-haired people have a quick temper' in terms of any study of how men and women differ.

Yet there are differences. Not of the order of 'all' and 'always' but 'usually' and 'probably'. One way of approaching this is not to take the wide term of 'men and women' but the narrower one of mother and father. If you observe the behaviour of parents generally, you find that there are different approaches to children and family life which can often be classed as mother's or father's approaches. I stress, not always, but often. The father's way, for example, in a difference of opinion, tends to be confrontation. He also likes rules to be kept. Mother tends to try to work things round so that the child does eat his carrot in the end, but without losing too much face. (After all, it does no harm to suggest that with cheese sprinkled on them they would be just what he wants. There is a subtle agreement that you have given a little and so he can too.) As a further development, this is usually labelled soft by father, who thinks it is better to be firm from the start.

I am being quite serious when I say that this is the kind of issue behind structuring the church by men and describing and representing God as male. Our response to mother and father is never quite the same. Therefore, although we may not always be able to describe the exact differences, we do need both male and female right through the life of the church. It will take a long time for this to happen and even longer than we might think, because for those women who are ordained or who are found in other capacities in the leadership of the church, the world in which they make decisions is already a male one, with that framework. The temptation is very strong to listen to those who tell you that 'of course you know that as a woman you will have to do better than a man to get on at all' and to try to be (for example) more aggressive, a more formidable chairman, a very unemotional pastor, because you feel it is the best way, whether consciously or even subconsciously. It will take a long time before women are relaxed enough to be themselves—and now, too, before men can relax after shrinking from the accusation of male chauvinist on every side. Only then will we be able to see what kind of difference it makes.

Now as I have said, Jesus has to have the body of male or female. What is interesting is to see in him what (at the risk of generalizing) you may call the female side. Rabbis did not deal with little children or with women, whereas he made a point of doing so. He wept. He would be gripped with compassion for the one individual in the midst of crowds and pressing concerns. He lived flexibly, responding to needs and situations as they arose. (A mother tends to live more in response to demands made upon her than in control of an already-determined set of lives.) We know instinctively of his power and authority, yet I think that men find it more difficult to explore his being also a victim. This is not to say that women are naturally the victim, but rather that in many societies they have been and still are the ones on the receiving end. In Jesus we see an identification with those who are not in control of the situation. He let himself be vulnerable. It is right that we understand and share in this quality of vulnerability.

The priest or minister has in the past had a good deal of his role cast for him as part of a semi-Christian society—whether he liked it or not. When we examine how much is convention and how much is essential to the gospel in that role then we also realize how much is convention about a male priest or minister. For example, it is said that people in a village could never see their vicar as a woman. This is mainly because in a village there is still a traditional vicar's role. It is like the way in which I have found that the content in which people are most reluctant to have a woman minister is their wedding. This is probably not so for your own church members who know you. It is other people who have a certain concept of how a church wedding should be. Even this is breaking down now, but when I have found this kind of feeling I have not tried to fight it. The conventional picture will change in time. Meanwhile, the important question is how much has this essentially to do with being a minister of the gospel. To me, many things that are traditionally functions of 'the vicar' may be for some the *bene esse* but they are certainly not of the *esse* of the ministry. Ordaining women sometimes helps to clarify what is happening in a way which has implications beyond the issue itself.

In describing working in a team, and in talking about the question of being a woman minister I have hinted at some of the personal strains behind the story. There *are* stresses that belong to different ministerial situations. There are also tensions that are likely to belong to any minister. Before I even started to train for the ministry, there were very real queries about the relevance of the church and the role of the minister in it and in society. But alongside that was the realization that if, after all, your work turned out to be relevant, to be worth-while, then you might very well be biting off more than you could chew.

This is put in another way in an article by Clifford Cleal, who says: 'Any Christian who tries to realise solidarity both with Christ and with "all sorts and conditions of men" is bound to experience tension, even suffering. A minister is no exception?'[9] I was beginning to realize something of this as 'any Christian' and I began to suspect that not only was a minister no exception, he or she might be thrust rather often into this position. Indeed, on the day of my ordination I wrote that I was numb and terrified.

The 'realisation of solidarity' seems to be about the minister's representative function. This is part of the ministry of all Christians, but the minister has been set aside to do it full time, and perhaps in a more concentrated way than other members are able to do. Being a representative person seemed to mean that you are to be 'ordinary', not in being the lowest common denominator kind of person, but in refusing to be set apart in a kind of clerical professionalism. At the time this chimed for me with the whispers I was hearing about it being good that the minister's status was being eroded. Being a woman meant that I started out with less status anyway! And in some ways more possibilities for being representative, in that people did not on the whole put up the kind of barriers that can happen when 'the minister's coming'.

Standing 'with Christ' means that as well as standing in strength you must know for yourself what it is to be weak. You will be given gifts of entering into suffering and sin, into doubt and temptation. Daniel Jenkins said that ministers must be so joined to Christ 'as to receive a glimpse of the meaning of his dereliction . . . He must know something of the depth and the agony and the infinite burden of the cosmic wounds of Christ by which we are healed.' He quotes P. T.

[9] Clifford Cleal, 'The Role of the Ordained Minister Today' *Baptist Quarterly*, Vol. XXV

Forsyth: 'We have to feed our life where all the tragedy of life is gathered to an infinite and victorious sacrifice in Christ. We are not the fire but we live where it burns.'[10]

Yes, we are to live where it burns. Where it burns with hope and joy, with warmth and light as well as with compassion, with the heat of the righteous ravaging of evil oppression, or with throbbing pain. If we live where it burns we are vulnerable. The light of the flame is always there, but so is the possibiliy of getting hurt.

It is at this point that your link with other people in ministry is vital; there is a sense in which you must do and bear alone, but in the Christian life community has always been an intrinsic part. The disciples were called into a group. Early Christian believing had the immediate corollary of joining together. I have mentioned team ministry as being very helpful. But there can be a danger sometimes in a team becoming over again a congregation. With or without a team, a minister's potential is cut down if there is a sense of his being separated from the church. (There are, of course, certain specialist ministries which operate like this, but even they often build up their own 'unofficial' church, or do in fact find it helpful to have a congregational base as well.) Theologically Baptist ministers believe that they are only members of the community, even though that community has set them apart for particular work. In practice sometimes we act as though being set apart gives us a right not to feel one with everyone else, and we talk of 'my people' as though we were somehow different.

Of course there are all kinds of reasons for this situation developing, not all on the minister's side, but it is a pity when it does. The minister needs to feel that he is a projection of a line that is already there, not a superior (or inferior) line of his own in another direction. It is only as he or she is part of a whole ministry has the right context for its full potential to be reached. The most fruitful directions in mission, in pastoral care, in worship will only be found if there are groups seeking together for them. Within the Christian community and its worship there may be tensions but there will also be the glimpse of the new Jerusalem to share, until the day when the crying and pain that you must now enter into will be no more.

[10] Daniel Jenkins, ibid., taken from Forsyth, P. T., *The Soul of Prayer*, Epworth Press

7

The Prospect of Ordination

Kenneth Wilson

Kenneth Wilson was born in 1937. Educated at Kingswood School, he read History and Divinity at Trinity Hall, Cambridge. His ministerial education began at Didsbury College, and has since continued in circuit in London and in Bath and while he was Chaplain at Kingswood School. He is Tutor in Philosophy at Wesley College, Bristol, and Part-time lecturer in the University of Bristol. He gave the Fernley-Hartley Lecture in 1973. His publications include *Making Sense of It* (1973), *Living It Out* (1975), and many articles and reviews.

Mr Wilson is married, with three children.

I have been fortunate in living amongst people, and in surroundings, where there has been the utmost encouragement to extend one's knowledge of what one already understood, and to take interest in new and exciting areas of human experience. Thus, while I was familiar with much of the region of Caernarvonshire and Anglesey (as it was then called), especially in the mountains, I never thought that its richness of mood or colour, its capacity to contribute to one's sense of belonging, could be exhausted. Yet, the prospect of a holiday in the Yorkshire Dales, or weekends in Birmingham, held for me just as much opportunity because there was the possibility of experience of something entirely new and different.

As a member of a small and fairly compact community in a provincial university town, my family had the acquaintance of people amongst whom we could find somebody knowledgeable about almost anything, or who could put one in contact with such a person. Since my father, a business man, had an abounding interest in everything and everybody, and a bold curiosity about the world, both in particular and general, our home was constantly full of guests and interesting conversation. The schools to which I went were not hidebound by any subservience to curricula, but were passionately committed to education. Thus at my preparatory school we were awoken by Beethoven, and persuaded of the virtues of Benjamin Britten; Homer was read to us (in Greek—so musical, you know!), Shakespeare and Chaucer unashamedly delighted in, but not to the exclusion of T. S. Eliot or Vachell Lindsay or playing rugby.

When I went to Kingswood School, my impression that there was nothing to fear in the world, that all knowledge was to be pursued, that curiosity was a virtue to be prized, and that beauty was an essential ingredient in any valuable human existence, was abundantly developed. I cannot remember a time when I have not read books, but at Kingswood it was assumed that anyone could read (and with application understand) a book on any topic. There was no attempt to restrict or confine. If one had some expertise, then one must explain it in a way that others could understand, if one had not, then one should cultivate a language, and a friendship, which would mean that one would become at home with it. Further, while what I have been talking about is undoubtedly an intellectual experience, it was also a personal experience; indeed I have come to think that the separation of these two is amongst the most dangerous things which can happen to a human being. For this I have to thank many influences, but principally A. B. Sackett, the Headmaster of Kingswood, and Christopher North, the Professor of Semitic Languages in the University College of North Wales, Bangor; both had a delight in creation, in the human imagination, and in language. They convinced me of the human importance of understanding the neurophysiology of the brain, and of the structure of matter, of reading novels, and of gaining familiarity with the history of the world. These were not merely areas in which a cultivated person might be expected to have some interest (though that is true), but awareness of them would make a difference to one's capacity to love and to be. Knowing these things made a difference to the knowing subject.

In thinking about what career to pursue I therefore had in mind opportunity to make use of a wide variety of interests. The three which came most obviosly to mind were business, medicine and the law. In each of these a high degree of technical skill and precise knowledge could only be made proper use of if it were combined with an increasingly wide general knowledge and committed interest. In business, for example, money is not of the first importance, people are; in medicine, technical skill (I fancied brain surgery!), is subservient to one's capacity to respond to the whole being of a patient's life; in the law, one can only employ one's legal expertise effectively if it is combined with a relentless pursuit of knowledge in any and every area. Language, in which I had an over-riding interest as a phenomenon, was obviously crucial in all of these areas, so that concern did not help me to decide. In the event I went to the university to read history, as a preparation for reading law, as I had decided that it was in the law that one had the opportunity to develop most of one's interests, and therefore the greatest capacity to contribute to one's society. Furthermore, the question of human rights had begun to concern me and I thought that the encouragement of a tradition of impartial justice was of central importance here. I envisaged myself as a Judge carefully listening, deliberating, and then guiding a jury, so that the precious gift of justice could be made real for all who needed it.

It may be wondered what all this has to do with the question of ordination, yet it was just these considerations which finally led me to offer as a candidate for the Methodist ministry. My family was Methodist, and of a traditionally Wesleyan variety. This above all implied three things, so far as we saw it. First, that the creation was good, to be loved and enjoyed. Secondly, that it was the context of God's real presence. Thirdly, that this presence was celebrated most significantly for the Christian in the eucharist. The untypical nature of this experience within existing Methodism should not hide the fact that it is in conformity with historical Methodism. A succession of ministers, relatives, and friends had given me some insight into what this might mean, at home and at school. But at the university I thought more consistently. A year at home, between school and university, had given me more opportunity to preach and take services more regularly as a local preacher (which I had been since I was sixteen), and this had required some deeper application. The further thought led me to the belief that the greatest single problem which a person or a community could have, concerned its lack of appreciation of the possibilities of meaning in life. This rootlessness of culture, of nation, or sex, colour and generation, led each to strive to secure his own interests at the expense of the other, and thus to perpetuate the illusion that no whole sense could be made of life, no whole response could be made to it. The three fundamental features of my Wesleyan heritage seemed relevant at this point. Were it the case that the creation was God's, and that it was the context of his active presence, and that the eucharist was a most significant way in which man celebrated that presence, and began to take part in his loving activity to perfect the world, then nothing could be more fundamental than encouraging men and women to consider these questions, and even if they did not, participating in the tradition oneself in order to preserve and develop it for the world's sake. Furthermore, it dawned on me with astonishing clarity and power, that no sort of activity could conceivably embrace so many skills, interests and attitudes. No matter what one was interested in, whether it be building one's own home, painting pictures, or dissecting frogs, it could all be done to the glory of God. What mattered was the encouraging of the excellence which God's commitment to the world obviously intended man to enjoy. On this analysis, there was needed a professional body of people set aside for reflection, for the teaching and interesting of others in the fact that this world with all its complexity, difficulty and delight was God's creation, and for pointing others to the usefulness of taking the life and death of Jesus seriously in such a reflection. Having met a girl who seemed to share the same sort of quest for wholeness, though from a different point of view, and with contrasting interests, the possibility of actually being a minister seemed worth considering. I did not know whether I had been called, but it seemed a good job, and since there was obviously a need for the profession, I decided to offer as a candidate. I was accepted.

I had only experienced the Church as the context of opportunity and fearless probing, though I knew through my reading that there were shameful periods in its history, and despicable people who had employed its institutions as the basis of personal power, in order to compensate for personal insecurity. However, I was surprised to be asked by a minister at my Synod why I was continuing in a secular university, rather than going straight to theological college. The thought had never occurred to me that secular and religious knowledge might be distinct, and that in accepting God one might be thought to be rejecting the created order. This was the first indication I received that the contemporary Church might not see itself as expressing in its worship the fundamental realities of the created order, but as trying to bring to the world something essentially alien to it; that it did not see itself as celebrating the essential presence of God in his world, but as trying to introduce him to it; that the Church did not see its task as bringing man into relationship with the world as God's creation, but as trying to rescue him from it. Indeed I was forced in the course of time to ask whether the Church did love the world as I believed God did, or whether it feared it; whether it accepted it, or rejected it; whether it served it or despised it.

My acceptance as a candidate, and the responsibility which it gave me in prospect, gave a fine definition to my concentration. I had to cultivate as much knowledge, sympathy, understanding and interest as I could. My tutors at theological college, where I began a research degree in philosophy, were entirely congenial and trustful. I was given every encouragement to read, write, reflect and discuss, which I seem to remember doing with tremendous gusto, long into the night. Thus it was with marvellous anticipation that I went to a city centre church as a probationer. That experience was a key factor in the development of my understanding of ordination.

There were five aspects of the work of the minister which seemed to me when I began to be of the utmost importance. There was first of all the Eucharist, in the celebration of which as a probationer I shared, but which, I am glad to say, I had no dispensation to celebrate. This was both the beginning and the end of it all, so far as I understood it, in the sense that in the activity of sharing the self-giving of God, we were embarking all over again on the task of working out what shape our giving of ourselves should take for the world in which we were set. It was both the real thing, and the shadow of what was to be; the mysterious 'now' of celebration was always the anticipated 'then' of fulfilment. It was both the earnest that all the parameters of hope would meet, and the harsh realization that they did not.

The second aspect was theology. Now theology is a discipline for which I find Christians have often less time than the educated non-Christian, and indeed the minister less time than the sensitive layman. Why this should be is itself an interesting matter for reflection. However, I was absolutely convinced that it was a vital feature of my work that I should continuously attempt to work out what it meant to claim that there was a God, and what belief in him could be held to imply for believers. Since I was assistant chaplain to the university Methodist Society, this may seem an obviously relevant matter, and it was indeed a pleasure to have so many questioning and doubting people around one to stimulate and share in reflection. But when I thought of theology I did not think of merely reading St Augustine and St Thomas, but of grasping the reality of God's activity wherever and whenever it was. For this an awareness of the ways in which theologians had tackled problems in the past was certainly useful, not to say necessary, but so also was a knowledge of contemporary administrative procedures, poetry and art, science and history, etc. For, as I saw my task, it was to employ the opportunity given to me for theological reflection to stimulate others to become aware of God for themselves, and not to pass on a secondhand system for reflection however well it might apparently have been thought out.

The task of theologizing was intimately related to the third aspect, which was pastoral care. In this the experience which contributed most to my understanding was the responsibilities which I had as a hospital chaplain. Since my task was to visit those who were not Church of England, Roman Catholic, or Jew, it can readily be seen that the numbers were both large and usually of no specific or recent Christian conviction. This was daunting in prospect, but in the event one of the most stimulating and revealing experiences of that short two years. Most people wanted to talk, most people were perplexed, most people had some clue as to the purpose that had brought my visit. Indeed the paradoxical fact dawned on me rapidly, that the conventional Christian believers had less understanding of the possible usefulness and purpose of a pastor than had the intelligent non-churchgoer. One of the reasons for this was undoubtedly that the church had domesticated and conventionalized the believer so that he could no longer doubt or grow, he could no longer search for what he had been led to believe he already had, whereas the nonbeliever was often puzzled, interested and determined in his search for meaning. Since the occasion of illness is hardly the time to take a person to task on their understanding of religion, it was frequently the case that one was of more use to the non-Christian than to the Christian.

The greatest single lack which a person can have is lack of curiosity, and lack of confidence to question. Curiosity has characterized the greatest human beings, both Christian and non-Christian; pastoral care involves at the very least the capacity to stimulate curiosity in others, and for this one must cultivate it in oneself. Many people are unable to develop any genuine curiosity in anything other than themselves, because they have not the language to make sense of their experience as they see it. Thus in talking with individuals, as a preliminary to genuine reflection and curiosity about the meaning of life, it may be necessary to spend time in conversation with the purpose of enabling the person concerned to find a coherent language for their experience. (In case the use of the term 'language' should mislead here, I should stress that I am not merely talking of words, but of the whole structure of word, concept, action and attitude by which a person expresses himself.) But it cannot be emphasized too strongly that such a task of counselling is merely a preliminary to the fundamental task of stimulating curiosity. Perhaps this is the contemporary understanding of 'convicting them of their sin', bringing people to an awareness of the fact that not to think, is not to be alive.

Administration was the fourth aspect of the task of the ordained person. It has always been a burden round our necks; some accept it with gratitude as a substitute for thought or genuine work, while others regard it as to be avoided at all costs because it interferes with 'the real work'. It is of course necessary. If one thinks of it simply as housekeeping, I think this helps. Housekeeping is not a full-time occupation (the fact that it is for many people is a matter for shame), it is what has to be done in order to be able to live; one cannot live without it. Therefore one must get it done with the minimum of fuss and time. The key to a responsible approach seems to lie in the recognition of the theological dimension of the task. For what one is striving to do is to plan the work of the church in society in such a way that both those who participate, and those who observe the activity of the church from outside, may be encouraged to dare to be puzzled and curious about the meaning of life, and be interested to think that, if they give attention to Jesus and the sorts of thoughts about life which those who have followed him have been provoked to entertain, they will find life more whole and fulfilling. An administrative process which is responsive to this theological dimension will always be subject to criticism,

and will be unlikely to be allowed to settle into any unde-
velopable pattern. Since the Church so often looks back,
rather than forward, its Lord would appear to be Lot, and its
institutions no more than a pillar of salt.

Lastly, I knew that I could not avoid preaching. And I did
not want to. In a sense, preaching was the public test of all that
has been said so far. Is any progress being made in the
understanding of God and the awareness of his presence
which we celebrate in the eucharistic feast? Is the pastoral
care which talks of making sense of life apparent in what is
being said? Is the structure of Church life reflecting the task of
stimulating curiosity? Or have we cast ourselves adrift from
the world on to a lonely sea preoccupied with our own fears,
looking for the Eternal Counsellor who will give his whole
attention to us, and to us alone? It was because I looked for
some sort of progress, and some sort of coherence of
response, that I always wrote out my sermons (I still do
usually), for there is nothing like the dead repetition in the
guise of spontaneity for encouraging isolation and illusion.
But we are not trying to pass on information in a sermon,
rather to give some clues about the worthwhileness of the
search for meaning and to encourage some to take an interest
in the clues many have found through giving attention to
Jesus. Preaching should take people for a walk, but leave
them to find their own way home; it should tell people a story,
but leave them to make up their own ending; it should disturb
contentment, and propose the possibility of a new peace.

There were many influences during this time, people and
books, paintings and plays. My superintendent minister, the
Rev. J. Neville Ward, shared my concern for literature and
art, and deepened it; his own profound understanding of the
spiritual life made me doubly aware that if I was to talk about
religion I must practise it, but that practising it was not possible apart from reflecting on it. This was most helpful to me in
the context of the 60s when so much criticism of the church
and of religion was not earthed in any significant understanding of theology, its task and purpose, or of the life of the
Christian community. It left one free to take what was good in
the criticism, and there was much that was good, without
being knocked over by the force of the gale.

Three books I remember in particular as taking me a step

on, two are philosophical and the third a volume of poetry. The first was Chomsky's *Ianua Linguarum*.[1] This was a stunning experience for me, not because of the strictly linguistic theory, though this is of course immensely interesting, but because of the possible philosophical implications of that theory. I had always been interested in language, but here was a theory which saw in language the crucial expression of human nature, and what is more one which assumed a fundamental, common structure for all possible natural languages. Furthermore, the common structure of language should be related to the fact that man has a common linguistic expectation for the world of his experience, and an innate and common linguistic sense which develops in response to this experience in the style of the community to which he had been born. Thus while each baby has the possiblity of learning any language, the innate linguistic sense expresses itself in the natural language of the community in which he is set. One feature in particular struck me, and that was Chomsky's remark how surprising it was that human beings could understand the sense of a sentence which they had never heard before; and utter sentences which they had themselves never heard before. This was a way in which potentially one might be able to hold together both a physical understanding of the brain and a non-behaviourist point of view. This excited me, for it emphasized the creative function of language, as opposed to its merely descriptive, or even its communicative purpose, while it nevertheless related this creativity to the physical structure of the brain.

The second book was by Thomas S. Kuhn, *The Structure of Scientific Revolutions*.[2] I had been puzzled by the question of how a fundamental set of assumptions about the nature of life could be tested or refuted; such a puzzle was natural for anybody who had been brought up with the problems of logical atomism and linguistic analysis, and the accusation of 'meaninglessness' laid at the door of any metaphysical statement. Having read *Honest to God*, I had been provoked to write a short article to the effect that the reason why it was possible to write such a bold and naïve book could only be

[1] Noam Chomsky, *Ianua Linguarum*, The Hague 1957

[2] Thomas S. Kuhn, *The Structure of Scientific Revolutions*, Chicago University Press, 1962; second enlarged edition, 1970

that theologians and believers had not worked at the task of understanding what they meant by the assertions they were making. Hence the assertions were not actually shown to be false, but implausible, which was much worse. Reading Kuhn gave much greater clarity to this idea. For he showed how a given understanding of the world, which he called a 'paradigm', gave plausibility to both the problems and the hypotheses of scientific research, and therefore how difficult it was to challenge the paradigm. After all, the paradigm cooked the books in its own favour to start with, by requiring that the problem be formulated in terms of the paradigm. However, although the world view, the paradigm, was not perhaps even disprovable, it ceased to be plausible, until eventually nobody took any serious notice of it when attending to real problems, even if it was necessary to pay lip service from time to time. The problem then became not so much a scientific question, as a sociological one, for it was the power-structure of scientific institutions which had to be attacked, rather than the truth or falsity of scientific theories. This whole process was analogous to the way in which a society came to the conclusion that existing realities no longer warranted accepted political institutions, and produced a consequent revolution.

This theory regarding developments in scientific understanding, seemed apt to the situation regarding theology. Nothing seemed clearer to me than that the traditional scheme of Christian religious reflection was implausible, as also the institutions which were based upon it. However, whereas it had once seemed essential to show this in some proof of falsification, I now realized that this was not possible, because one was continually required to formulate the questions in terms which assumed the truth of the intellectual structure one was attempting to question. Therefore the task was to work with renewed attention and concentration upon a new set of statements of what Christian faith actually amounted to. Limits traditionally imposed upon such restatements had to be resisted. For example, while it was plausible to suggest that anything which counted as Christianity in the second half of the twentieth century should be consistent with what had earlier been regarded as such, this presumed that we knew how to interpret the earlier history of the Church. Whereas, it is important to realize that it may be only some future development which shows the significance of the past. Pillars of salt do have a habit of frustrating progress, if one keeps turning round to see whether one is safe. What is required is a contemporary systematic theology, but whether such a thing is possible, and if so what form or forms it should take, is a matter for debate. Such a theology will take seriously the actual understanding of the world which human disciplines offer to us, and the social, political, economic and personal context in which people live. Relevance is, after all, a necessary condition of plausibility.

A third book was of quite a different kind. It was *Pieta* by the Welsh poet R. S. Thomas.[3] It is to be expected that a person interested in language will be attracted by poetry, and indeed I was. For a poet attempts to express a mood, an idea, a scene or a situation, in words, while not imprisoning it and thus making it impenetrable. To the extent that he moulds it into too tight or exact a structure, he impedes its power to communicate and open others to new feelings and ideas with regard to their own experience. On the other hand, too loose a structure, or vague and lax linguistic usage, may leave a poem entirely malleable by the reader, and thus communicate nothing to him except what he already knows. R. S. Thomas has a most exact use of language, combined with a delicate eye for structure which means that he engages the reader in the hard, relentless search for meaning in life, indeed for life itself. The discipline required of any would-be searcher is finely expressed in an ever-increasing tautness of language, and paring down of the structure; but it is not a destructive discipline, for combined with it is a rare delight in human sensitivities and skills pressed into images which grasp and provoke tired imaginations. Whereas sciences, whether natural or social, and the so-called arts disciplines of history and literature, tend to concentrate interest upon aspects of the use of language, poetry itself employs language as a means whereby we may attempt to grasp the whole. It seemed to me, that whatever the interest of aspects of life, one can never as a Christian, and therefore *a fortiori* as an ordained person, lose hold of the worthwhileness of the attempt to grasp the whole. Reductionism is a valid methodology by which to develop

[3] R. S. Thomas, *Pieta*, Hart-Davis, 1966

clarity of thought but it can never be the stance of the Christian, though this remark must be seen to be independent of the question of the truth of reductionism.

There are many poems by R. S. Thomas which could be quoted with pleasure, but let me give just one, because its insight is so clear, and obvious.

In Church

Often I try
To analyse the quality
Of its silences. Is this where God hides
From my searching? I have stopped to listen,
After the few people have gone,
To the air recomposing itself
For vigil. It has waited like this
Since the stones grouped themselves about it.
These are the hard ribs
Of a body that our prayers have failed
To animate. Shadows advance
From their corners to take possession
Of places the light held
For an hour. The bats resume
Their business. The uneasiness of the pews
Ceases. There is no other sound
In the darkness but the sound of a man
Breathing, testing his faith
On emptiness, nailing his questions
One by one to an untenanted cross.[4]

The reality of ordination lies in the requirement to puzzle, to search, to be curious; one is not on the inside, but at the perimeter; one is neither protected, nor protective, but trying to understand the impossibility of telling the whole story in a silent, empty world. And yet one has something to go on, there is not just nothing, there is one's own breathing. What is the significance of that? What does it mean? The idea that such questions form moulds into which traditional theologies will pour without remainder is nonsense. Yet equally nonsensical is the suggestion that past responses of men and women

[4] Ibid., p. 44

162

to analogous situations are irrelevant to our present understanding.

A move to Kingswood School, which when it began was
combined with the care of three churches in the Bath Circuit,
gave me the opportunity to test some of these reflections in a
specialized context. Education is not now, if it ever has been,
an easy world for Christianity; the accusation of indoctrina-
tion is all too readily levelled at some approaches to Christian
education, and sometimes justified because of the protective
attitude which is encouraged to flourish in regard to specific
theological systems, or supposed 'truths'. In going to Kingswood I was certainly not going into any such environment.
There was a genuine freedom to think, and encouragement to
be curious. But amongst some pupils, and perhaps some
parents therefore also, there were two underlying and con-
flicting assumptions. First, it was thought that any opinion
was as good as any other if the subject in question did not lend
itself to absolutely certain, definitive conclusions. Since the
context of society in which one lived was one of extreme
individualized forms of freedom, it was sometimes difficult to
encourage attention to the sort of discipline of thought which
would enable progress to be made in understanding even
when absolutely certain answers were impossible. Secondly,
the difficulty was compounded by the beginnings of that
conservative backlash which has frustrated and does frustrate
the possibility of thought, by imposing an invariable system,
whether theological, historical, political or logical. The ease
with which consistency of thought and intellectual rigour may
be undermined by confusing it with the frustration of personal
liberties must constantly be borne in mind; the opposite is in
fact the case, there is no freedom apart from careful attention
to argument and thought. Equally fallacious is the argument
which sees logical truth and consistency of argument as
associated only with one system of reflection. In this as in so
many other areas of life it is the quality of the chasing which
counts, for there is no arriving.

Above all, the experience showed me how creative and
affectionate human kind can be, how responsive to encouragement of relationship and physical environment, and how
high the expectations are which we have of one another.
These expectations have to be high or we give up the stimulus
of criticism and optimistic debate. It was also a healthy

community in which discussion was usually and happily free from personal reductionism which the weak employ in order to gain power, while losing arguments. These are the destructive tactics which deal more with the motives a person has in holding a point of view, than with the plausibility and the validity of the argument employed in its support. Disagreements therefore were valid disagreements in the face of difficulty and perplexity, which had to be examined for the strength of the respective point of view, rather than mere personal whim. Furthermore, the strength of colleagueship and mutual support of an institution which we believed could be made to serve the best interests of all those who constituted it, was deep and abiding. It provided, and of course still provides, a context in which all members can begin to explore what it might mean to serve church and state. The motto of the school, is *In Gloriam Dei Optimi Maximi in Usum Ecclesiae et Republicae.*

One other comment on that experience is apposite before coming to the present situation of the Church and what we hope for from ordained persons. There was no way in which a chaplain in such a place could convince himself that he understood things better, or could do things better, than any other member of the staff. There was no possibility of justly claiming that he taught all the religious studies in the school, for literature, art, physics and history—not to mention geography, geology and every other element in the development of linguistic skills for the interpretation of human experience—all of them, in so far as they were true, illuminated human possibilities and defined expectations for man in God's world. Somehow the theologian had to act so as to encourage the confidence of others, not to threaten it, to make free and not to obligate. That opportunity seemed to be preserved by the context of worship, and above all by the celebration of the Eucharist, in which the minister as celebrant is standing for that Unknown Other, whom he must separate from every known understanding and every proposed scheme, if there is ever to remain the possibility that mankind may understand. In this sense I became even more aware than I had been before, that ordination must in some sense or another be understood as objective. It represents in personal form the fact that there is something to be understood, to be responded to, to come to terms with. It seems best here to use the notion of objectivity, with all its difficulties, rather than separation, for by now it will be abundantly clear that ordination does not involve separation at all. Objectification, on the other hand, holds together the need to present within the community the reality of what is to be sought, while not encouraging the one who objectifies this for the community to believe that he himself is not also in need of exactly the same symbolic objectification. Hence the objectification which I am talking of in connection with the ordained person, is no more and no less than the objectification which is presented by the church for the whole world in the eucharistic activity. It is no more done by clergy by themselves, than it is by the laity; no more done by the living alone, than by the dead; it is on each and every occasion, done by all believers, the whole Christian community, with the delightful presence of God.

It seemed therefore to me, that a minister objectified the freedom that man had to think, not to be conditioned by the structure of thought which he inherited, and to be constantly surprised by the sheer fact of the existence of things. Always some new thought, some new attitude, some new insight, could awaken man again with renewed vigour to tackle the pressing, but not depressing, problems with which he found himself involved. There is no problem, no situation and no difficulty, which it is not possible to think of a way of making better, however little; perhaps this is the essential significance of the Christian doctrine of resurrection. To take this point further, one could argue that the task of the Church, and *a fortiori* therefore, of the minister, is to reject all inevitabilities and to point to the constant possibility of responsible choice.

It is not an unfamiliar thought that God's purpose in creating, is to enable the emergence of personal being, through a growing responsiveness on the part of creation to God's presence. We have ourselves, in our relationships with one another some inkling of what such personal being may be, for there are those with whom we find ourselves completely at home and free, and others who by their grasping insecurity seek to control and humiliate. Most people would like to be open and courteous in their dealings with others, but most of us, if not all, find that such approaches meet with rebuff, indifference, or exploitation. Hence the tendency to circumscribe human life, to draw in one's horns, and to settle for what can be done without risk of too much pain. This frequent individual reaction has found a social context recently through the anxiety about the economic and political future of the world. Is the fact that there is a scarcity of vital resources consistent with the view that the world can sustain genuine personal life of the kind men want? Is the growing totalitarianism of governments resistable by individuals who desire freedom, or does the mere survival of man as a species require such a limitation of individual freedom, that the concept of personal maturity is no more than of historical interest? Against all such talk, Christian faith asserts the reality and reasonableness of personal life.

But what of the inevitabilities of systems? What, for example, of the inevitabilities of the way in which we organize our economic life together? This is just the sort of example we need to keep in mind, for there are no inevitabilities about systems as a whole, even if there are within systems. Economic systems are man-made accounts of how we organize our economic relationships with one another; they are therefore essentially structures for which we can take responsibility, and about which we can in principle make choices. This is clearly not the context to debate what sort of choices should be made, though two pertinent points may be made. There is no one system which can be called 'Christian' to the exclusion of every other. Neither capitalism, nor socialism, for example, could of itself be called the truly Christian economic system. Secondly, any economic system which makes it impossible for an individual to realize his whole person in relationships with others, is to be opposed by the Christian community. This in itself offers the church a task of analysis and judgement. What sorts of economic system enhance the possibility of human relationships, and what sorts limit them, threaten to diminish them, or destroy them?

The same point should be made with regard to individuals in their own lives. What are the structures of thought, of attitude and assumption, which frustrate the possibility of growing personal responsiveness and commitment? There are no inevitabilities here either. A broken marriage, the loss of business opportunities, the death of a child, inordinate success, none of these things is utterly or necessarily destructive of the possibility of a person's whole maturity. If (and I admit that it is 'if'—but the truth and falsity of Christian faith cannot be argued here) the Christian tradition is correct in affirming that the world owes its nature and potential to a God who wills personal wholeness for the individual and therefore for society too, then the task of the Church will always be to identify what in any given time and place limits the fulfilment of that potential, and to commit all its energy to opposing it.

But the means which the Church employs to oppose them involves the consistent attempt to reform and develop its own structures and understanding so as to present, in cogent and creative example, what in fact it is proclaiming. Here the position of the ordained person becomes crucial. He is required to criticize and evaluate the life of the church so that it can perform this task, for the very same limits which threaten personal maturity within society at large, threaten it too within the church. To keep the church open to its opportunities which it believes flow from the nature of the world as created by God, it is necessary that it constantly be subject to judgement. Hence it needs to be affirmed with passionate concern, that there are no theological systems, no structures of church organization, whether national, local or of a world-wide kind, which are the truth, or which should be regarded as the inevitable form for the truth of faith. On the contrary churches, and individual Christians, must learn to take responsibility for these systems and to see them as human constructions to account for aspects of human experience at given periods of human history. Theological systems cannot therefore be imposed, as if they were revealed by a God, but must be worked at, criticized, and even discarded if they do not enliven man's present awareness of the opportunities of personal living.

No person, whether he be ordained or not, can fulfil such a role on behalf of man in society, or for the Christian community, unless he or she sees himself or herself as under judgement too. The ordained person is just as likely as any other person to attempt to impose personal interests and project personal inadequacies upon the life of the church. And in this case, of course, to produce no justified comment on the limits to actual experience implicit within a given society, except by accident. Only if the ordained person sees the possibility of new insight, and the possible wholeness of things, and works with others for the personal expression of this within his own life will he gain any experience of what it is to be engaged in the activity of becoming free. The vulnerability which this demands offers the constant temptation to laziness, indifference, or thoughtless activity. The latter is undoubtedly the most dangerous and the most common feature of Christian life today.

The task of the ordained person is therefore threefold. First, the symbolical presentation by his relationship with the Christian community, of the objectivity of the task to which all men are called; the fulfilment of the potential of God's creative activity, through relationship with God himself. This symbolic proclamation presented by ordination, is thus not a matter of privilege for the ordained person himself, but a representative act, whereby the Christian community expresses its belief in the ultimate nature of man, as a being born for communion with God. This communion is celebrated above all in the Eucharist, which proclaims the perfection and unity of all created things through the grace of God. Confidence about this as the reality for man, is traced with greater or lesser plausibility to the life, death and teaching of Jesus, so that it is naturally reflection on him that is built into the eucharistic celebration.

The objectivity of this proclamation about man, through the symbolic act of ordination, and through the celebration of the communion of man and God in the Eucharist is vital, because experience and inclination so often persuade man to give up the struggle to make a reality of this insight in life. Hence the significance of the fact that the Eucharist must be seen as both complete and potential, actual and provisional. What we celebrate will, paradoxically, not happen if we do not think about it. So, the second task of the ordained person is to think, and to think as openly and responsibly as he can about the meaning of what is symbolized by ordination and by the celebration of the Eucharist. What does it mean to be, 'made in the image of God'? What does it mean that man can know God? What does it mean when the same word, 'person', is used to refer to the ultimate reality of both God and man? Of course answers to these questions can be quoted from Christian theological traditions, of wildly differing kinds, but that is merely to adduce some of the raw material necessary for thinking now. For we do not want to know only what such statements were thought to mean, but what they might mean now, or even whether these are the sort of questions which men find it sensible to ask now. In his thinking, the ordained person begins to take responsibility therefore for what he thinks, and not merely to quote, or live at the passive level of reflection.

One way of putting this task would be to say that it requires the capacity to wonder. The concept of wondering combines within it both the notion of astonishment and a consequent doubt or curiosity, which is the *sine qua non* of learning. Ministers who cease to wonder are easily domesticated and secularized; are likely to view the church as a place of safety and security away from the pressures of the world, rather than as a frontier of reflection and judgement. In a time of anxiety for the future of the church, congregations may prefer such people, for they will offer the apparently pleasant diversion of activity without thought. Ministers who develop the capacity to wonder, however, will not be able to keep it to themselves; they will want the insights, experience and participation of all. From this it follows that the second task of the minister, to think, can only be fulfilled for him if he is encouraging others to think for themselves. This is the very opposite of what has sometimes been assumed, but is essential to the maturity of persons in relationship. The truth cannot be given to another person, it can only be discovered by a person for himself; only if this is so indeed, can we begin to understand what it is to be responsible for the way in which we think, and for what we think.

One consequence of this is that hierarchical structures which want to hand down ideas, and which are not responsive to the ideas, interests and concerns of those who individually constitute the structure, are unlikely to be contexts for the development of personal maturity, for they work to deny the possibility of responsibility, for all except the few. Ministers need to be aware of the ways in which by depending upon the ecclesiastical structure to support them, they are frustrating the communication of the meaning which they symbolize by their ordination. Clearly the education of ministers is a vital matter here.

The third task is work. Such a naive sentence may seem too obvious, but I do not think it can be or one would not see such confusion in the understanding of whether a minister should work for the church, or for the world. Work is made up of all that activity which makes a reality of, and therefore gives shape to, the claim of Christians that this is God's world and that he asks man to share responsibility for it with him. It is constituted of all that expresses the ultimate perfection of man, and the fulfilment of God's purpose in creation. Thus preaching, which invites man to understand that he can accept responsibility, or gardening, which offers the opportunity of disciplined production, or scientific enquiry which opens up new awareness of the natural order, or a poem which challenges a person's aspirations, all of these things may be work. The task of the ordained person, if he has any special work, is to gather all these activities together in his imagination, and to reflect upon them, so that all may see how and in what way they are contributing to man's awareness that he shares with God responsibility for the world.

This 'special' activity should not be made too much of, or he may end up by thinking that although everybody does little bits, he is the only person who does the whole thing. As if while others were scrummaging, kicking, tackling and falling, he was the only one who was actually playing rugby. This is not so. It therefore seems vital that the structure of the church should not operate in such a way as to shield ordained persons from the ordinary work of living. Perhaps we should move towards a situation where ministers are given a higher remuneration for their work, and expected to take sole responsibility for their accommodation. The present arrangement encourages a dependence, and even a sense of not being responsible. The key understanding of the special nature of the ordained person's work is in what he symbolically presents by the very fact of his ordination, and by the work which he does in celebrating the wholeness and perfection of all things in the Eucharist.

These three tasks, symbolic statement of the Christian

understanding of man, thinking, and working, are so vague, and intentionally so, that no ordained person can ever free himself from the obligation to ask himself what exactly it means to be doing what he is doing and to be what he is. That basic question will necessarily remain if he is to enable the church (of which he is but a part) to exercise its ministry.